The Absolute Guide to Dashboarding & Reporting with Power BI

by

Kasper de Jonge

Holy Macro! Books
PO Box 541731, Merritt Island, FL USA

Author: Kasper de Jonge

Tech Reviewer: Adam Saxton

Publisher: Bill Jelen

Compositor: Jill Cabot

Cover Design: Alexander Philip

Indexing: Nellie J. Liwam

Published by: Holy Macro! Books, PO Box 541731, Merritt Island, FL 32954 USA

Distributed by: Independent Publishers Group, Chicago, IL

First Printing: February 2019. Printed in USA

ISBN Print 978-1-61547-057-0,
    Mobi 978-1-61547-140-9,
    PDF 978-1-61547-240-6,
    ePub 978-1-61547-363-2

Library of Congress Control Number: 2019930607

Contents

Preface v

Acknowledgments ix

1 - Introduction 1

2 - Understanding Dashboards and Reports 5

3 - Collecting and Preparing the Data 11

4 - Building the Main Report 45

5 - Building Detailed Reports 89

6 - Sharing Dashboards and Reports Within an Organization.......................................119

Index of Tips 143

Index 145

Preface

The first version of this book focused on using Power Pivot and Excel for dashboarding and reporting. After I finished that book in 2014, I was determined not to write another one: Writing a book is hard ☺. As the popularity of Power BI rose, Bill Jelen nudged me to write a new version of the book, focusing now on using Power BI for dashboarding and reporting, but I put it off. Now, almost four years after *Dashboarding and Reporting with Power Pivot and Excel* was published, I am nearing completion of *Dashboarding and Reporting with Power BI*.

What made me decide to finally update the book? Well, frankly, Power BI is now ready for it. Over the past couple of years, we on the Power BI team have created a new product from scratch, and it finally has all the features needed to re-create Excel dashboards and reports—but with Power BI. Another great motivator is the fact that I am still getting great feedback on the first edition of the book.

I have been in and out of the business intelligence industry for the past 15 years. These years have brought fundamental shifts in the way we work. We have gone from full-fledged IT-centric reporting to now enabling business users to work together with IT and also enabling everyone in an organization to work with data.

When I met Power Pivot in 2009, I immediately fell in love. As soon as I installed the first beta of Power Pivot, I knew the business intelligence world that I worked in would change forever. Now that Power BI has come along, it is possible to create insights without being a business intelligence professional; you just need to be familiar with Excel. BI professionals and business users alike are enthusiastic for Power BI.

I hope you will find this book very useful in creating dashboards that provide insights into data, and I'm looking forward to seeing you out there in the Power BI community. You can find me at my blog, **http://www.kasperonbi.com**, and on Twitter, at **http://twitter.com/kjonge**.

How I Got Started with Power BI

Today I work on the Microsoft BI team, which creates amazing tools that allow every Excel and business user in the world to gain insights into data. This is the story of how my love of Power Pivot brought me to work at Microsoft.

I have been passionate about computers and IT from the moment my parents bought me a Commodore 64 in 1988. When I started going to a school that focused on IT, I actually started paying attention, and my grades finally started going up. Ever since then, I have been glued to computers.

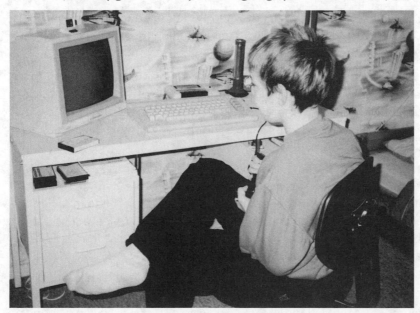

"Working" on my Commodore 64 in 1988. Look at that wallpaper.

My first jobs were not in crunching data or getting numbers to people using Excel. I was riding the tail end of the dot-com bubble in the late 1990s, building websites. I've always had an affinity for trying to make sense of large amounts of data, but I had no idea there was a whole world out there that did this for a living—or that it had a name. I fondly remember that somewhere along the line, I tried to use HTML and SQL Server 6.5 to create a report that contained several charts. I continued going down the development path, using SQL, .NET, and ASP.NET while living in the weapon of choice for every developer: Visual Studio.

In 2004 I made a career switch to a DBA/developer role, where I was introduced to data warehousing. I was hooked. Here I was also introduced to the tools that go on top of data warehouses, such as Cognos PowerPlay, which allows users in a business to analyze the data in their organization. I realized that, thanks to BI tools, users were able to get their own profound new insights. They were enthusiastic about being able to work with such data for the first time.

When I decided I wanted to see some different companies, I tried my hand at consulting and moved back into a developer role. But I kept trying to get work that allowed me to give data to users in any shape or form. After about two years, I wanted back into business intelligence and managed to talk my manager into sending me off to an Analysis Services course. That five-day crash course in building multidimensional models was my introduction to Microsoft BI. After that, I largely focused on using cubes and reports to build BI solutions, as well as on occasional data warehouse jobs. I became a typical BI developer, working on long projects to deliver value to business users who usually had to wait some time to get the data they needed. They often came to my desk, asking for new calculations or additions to the models because they did not have the capability or tools to do it themselves. I wasn't really an Excel user, but I worked closely with business users (typically ones who did use Excel) to make sure they got the information they needed. While I was doing this work, I also started blogging, mostly to keep track of my findings for later reference. I still maintain that blog, at **http://www.kasperonbi.com**.

One day in late 2008, I heard about a new project called Gemini that would allow business users to gather and analyze their own data directly inside Excel (see **http://ppivot.us/SEUSO**). I was intrigued with this revolutionary technology that would bring the power of the complex cubes world directly to Excel users. This new product would make it possible for anyone to use Excel to load millions of rows of data from multiple different places and combine the result into one report with ease. It seemed like science fiction to me then.

In August 2009, I finally got a chance to play with Gemini (**http://ppivot.us/O1NUW**). I was awed and in love: Gemini made it easy to quickly build reports that had before taken hours.

Then, in November 2009, my eyes were really opened, when I was introduced to the language that was underneath it all: DAX (**http://ppivot.us/v3ThX**), an incredibly powerful language that enables users to do a lot with ease.

Around the same time, I found a partner in my Power Pivot explorations: Rob Collie (**http://ppivot.us/aqdx8**). We spent many nights trying to figure out how Power Pivot worked and trying to find cool new things we could do with it. It was a pretty amazing time. I started trying to convince my manager that Power Pivot was a great tool and that we should use it in our day-to-day work with customers—and I was starting to get traction.

In June 2010, I attended TechEd in New Orleans. Rob Collie and many other folks from the Microsoft product team were there, too. The conference was a frenzy of Power Pivot discussions. It seemed like this was the only thing the entire BI community could talk about. I had many discussions with Rob about Power Pivot, and near the end of TechEd, Rob said, "I'm leaving Microsoft. Why don't you take my job at Microsoft? I think you would do great." I was stunned. I'd never thought that was possible and dismissed the idea pretty quickly.

After some talks with my wife, I decided to send Microsoft my resume. A few weeks later, I was interviewing with the team, and about four months later, I worked my first day at Microsoft, helping designing features for Power Pivot for SQL Server 2012. I was able to make a living working on the product I love. Pretty awesome!

Notes and Tips

This book covers a lot of different topics, written as a story about a user named Jim. Throughout the story, I often dive deeply into various subjects, call out certain areas, and give tips. To do this without deviating from the story, I make heavy use of notes as well as tips that fall into four categories:

- Data Model Tip
- Visualization Tip
- Power BI Tip
- Power BI Desktop Tip

At the end of the book, I provide an index of all these tips so you can easily find them at any time.

Hyperlinks

Throughout the book, I reference sites and blog posts for further reading, including my blog, Kasper on BI, Microsoft online help, and others. Because hyperlinks can be very long, I have used a URL-shortening tool to create shortened links, such as **http://ppivot.us/SEUSO** rather than **http://www.powerpivotblog.nl/ project-gemini-building-models-and-analysing-data-from-excel-memory-based-dimensional-model/**. If you are reading a physical copy of this book, make sure you pay attention to the capitalization as you type the URLs because they are case sensitive.

Samples, End Results, and Data Sources

This book describes how to build reports and dashboards based on a Microsoft Access database. Some readers might find it valuable to follow along with the book and build the project themselves, and others might want to see and play with the end result themselves. I have therefore uploaded all files to my website for you to download: **http://ppivot.us/sampl32d**. All the measures used in this book are available at **http://ppivot.us/daxfile**.

Acknowledgments

A book is never written alone, and so many people contributed to this book in both small and big ways that it's nearly impossible to write a complete list. Many users of Power BI both inside and outside Microsoft, bloggers, tweeps, conference attendees, and, of course, the Power BI development team helped me shape the book.

Of course, there are some people I need to especially thank for their help because without them, I wouldn't even be in the position to write a book. I thank Rob Collie for putting me on this crazy journey in 2009, when we were trying to understand DAX during the Project Gemini timeframe and he urged me to change my life by going to work for the Analysis Services team and moving to Redmond.

I also have to give thanks to the true masters of DAX—Howie Dickerman, Srinivasan Turuvekere, Jeffrey Wang, and Marius Dumitru—for creating DAX in the first place and helping me each time the DAX became too magical. Finally, I thank Adam Saxton for helping out by doing a tech review and getting rid of those pesky bugs.

This book wouldn't have been possible without the help of Bill Jelen as publisher, Kitty Wilson for editing, and Alexander Philip for the awesome cover design.

Finally, I want to thank my family, Mom and Dad, for getting it all started with that first Commodore 64. And of course I thank my beautiful girls—Anouk, Karlijn, and Merel—for putting up with my crazy passions and allowing me to spend time away from them.

1 - Introduction

This book is a follow-up to my earlier book, *Dashboarding and Reporting with Power Pivot and Excel*, which covers building reports and dashboards using Power Pivot for Excel. Now, four years later, the book you're currently reading shows how to build reports and dashboards using Power BI instead. This book is a little different from most books already out there on Power BI. It doesn't cover all the features of Power BI, nor does it cover the DAX language extensively. Many other books do those things well. A few good examples are Bill Jelen's *PowerPivot for the Data Analyst*, Rob Collie's *DAX Formulas for PowerPivot*, and Matt Allington's *Super Charge Power BI: Power BI Is Better When You Learn to Write DAX*.

This book is intended as a very practical book to help you get started on a Power BI journey and bring your data analysis skills to the next level. This book follows Jim, a business user who is very familiar with Excel, on his journey to create a financial dashboard and complementary reports in Power BI. The journey starts with Jim finding out what information his organization needs to understand the current rhythm of its business. He then gathers the needed data for presentation in a dashboard, for which he must determine the best ways to visualize the information. As you follow Jim on this journey, you will use Power BI Desktop and DAX formulas to solve several very common business calculations, such as year-to-date revenue, variance-to-target, and year-over-year growth.

You will also watch as Jim creates reports in Power BI Desktop to allow those in his business to dive deeper into the numbers. Then you'll see how to share those workbooks using Power BI.

In many places, this book dives deeply into subjects such as the Power BI analytical engine, DAX formulas, and Power BI and dashboard design tips and tricks.

What Is Business Intelligence?

Before you get hands-on with Power BI, it's important to look at why the tools discussed in this book even exist.

Business intelligence (*BI*) has traditionally been used as an umbrella term to refer to software and practice that should lead to better insights and decisions for an organization. Instead of making decisions based on gut feeling, an organization can base its decisions on actual facts it visualizes by using business applications. Many Excel professionals are likely to think, "Hey, that's what I'm doing every day, but I don't give it a fancy name!"

BI gained traction in the 1990s, when companies started creating and collecting more and more data but couldn't get the information into the hands of the business users to create insights and make decisions based on that information.

Building BI solutions has traditionally been the territory of IT organizations and consulting firms. It has often resulted in very heavy-weight and expensive projects that are highly curated and complex.

A *data warehouse* collects data from all over a company and consolidates it into what many think of as "the single version of the truth" for data. An IT organization may want all data to flow through the BI system to make sure it's consistent and non-redundant, in order to gain "correct" insights.

To make the data in a data warehouse actionable, organizations have often created *cubes* on top of the data warehouses. They have optimized those cubes to gain fast access to the data for doing quick analytics on large amounts of data. Then, on top of those cubes, canned reports are created to help users get insights into the data. In the 2000s, Excel improved this situation with the addition of PivotTables, which allow users to drag and drop data from a cube straight into Excel.

Today, the stream of information that flows through an organization comes not just from BI systems but also from cloud-based solutions like Microsoft Dynamics, Salesforce, and Internet of Things devices, as well as, of course, the number-one BI tool in the world: Excel. Users from the business side of an organization—without help from the IT side—can create reports directly at the source. These reports often bypass a BI solution completely or mash up data from the data warehouse with additional data retrieved from sources such as the ones just mentioned. This often leads to clashes between IT and business users because IT folks want the data to come from their BI solution, but the business cannot wait for IT to provide that information. The world does not stand around and wait for data to become available. Events happen all the time, and it is often crucial for an organization to react quickly.

As the pace of the world has increased and as more and more data has become available to organizations, CFOs and other stakeholders in organizations have wanted to get insights into data more and more quickly. BI was traditionally set to create insights through long projects, but that type of system makes it hard to quickly get insights into the ever-changing data. When and after the financial crisis hit in 2007–2009, the business world had to make many cutbacks, especially in the IT space. So, at the same time that IT departments were being expected to provide oversight of and more insights into data, they were being given fewer resources they could use to consolidate larger amounts of data.

But an organization doesn't need to rely on just its IT department for data. An army of business users in any organization know Excel and also know the data inside out, and they are very proficient at creating reports and using data to gain insights. Microsoft recognized this and thought that perhaps business users and IT could work together to serve the information needs of the organization and use each other's strengths instead of competing. In 2006, Microsoft began an incubation project called Gemini, named for the constellation. The twins in this project are IT and business users, working together.

Microsoft started its BI journey in 1994 by creating the very successful product Microsoft SQL Server Analysis Services (SSAS), which is designed for developers with an IT background. It is the best-selling analytical database engine in the industry. The idea behind Gemini was to shape the world-leading BI product SSAS into something that fits in Excel and can be used by Excel professionals. The Gemini incubation team aimed to determine whether it would be possible to empower Excel professionals and at the same time have them work together with IT. The team wanted to figure out how to put more business intelligence into the hands of the business users and allow them to "self-serve" the information.

The Gemini team determined that it needed to create a product with a few radical features:

- **The ability to work with massive amounts of data:** Since SSAS had hit the market in 1994, a lot had changed in the IT industry. Importantly, PCs had gotten more powerful, and memory had gotten much cheaper. For the Gemini team, this meant that the product would need to work on the data and optimize it for analytics use in Excel. Whereas Excel 2010 and earlier allowed a user to work with 1 million rows of data, the Gemini team wanted a product that would allow users to work with very very large amounts of data directly in Excel—much larger amounts of data than anyone could have dreamed of before. The team thought that working with 200 million rows of data should be like a walk in the park.
- **The ability to create a single PivotTable that combines data from two separate tables without writing a single VLOOKUP():** One of the most common uses of Excel is combining data from several separate data sources into a single report. In traditional Excel, you need to use the complicated Excel function VLOOKUP to combine the data into a single table. In Power Pivot, you can leave the data in separate tables and just create a relationship.
- **The Data Analysis Expressions (DAX) language:** DAX, which is designed for analytics, is based on the Excel formula language and even shares some functions with Excel. At the same time, it's very different from the Excel formula language: Whereas the Excel formula language references cells in a worksheet, DAX references tables and columns.

These three changes together have brought a lot of power to the fingertips of many Excel users. As Bill Jelen (also knowns as MrExcel) describes in his book *PowerPivot for the Data Analyst* (**http://ppivot. us/5Vqxd**), "There are two types of Excel users: People who can do a VLOOKUP with their eyes closed and everyone else....Suddenly, hundreds of millions of people who (a) know how to use a mouse and (b) don't know how to do a VLOOKUP are able to perform jaw-dropping business intelligence analyses."

Project Gemini wanted to bring the power of SSAS to a billion users of Excel—right on their desktops. This is referred to as "personal BI" or "self-service BI." But project Gemini was meant to be more than an add-in for Excel. It was meant to provide "team BI" so that a workbook shared with team members using Share-Point would retain all the interactivity but could be used by many users at the same time, through a web browser—no Excel required. The idea was that the data in a workbook could be refreshed via an automated schedule so that new data would be added to the workbook with no work needed. Another benefit of sharing workbooks to SharePoint would be that it would allow IT to govern the data shared onto Share-Point.

In October 2009, Gemini was renamed *PowerPivot for Excel*, and it first shipped with Excel 2010 (**http://ppivot.us/5Vd7u**). It was quite clear that PowerPivot would radically change both business intelligence and Excel. Shortly after the release of Excel 2013, Microsoft added a space to the tool's name—*Power Pivot* (**http://ppivot.us/ifdYe**). Power Pivot today is still available for Excel 2010, Excel 2013, and Excel 2016. However, in Excel 2016, the name Power Pivot disappeared, and the functionality, which remains the same, became a native part of Excel.

Microsoft's latest entrant in the BI world, Power BI, was released in 2015. Built on the success of Power Pivot, Power BI has truly revolutionized the business intelligence world. Whereas business users were the primary audience for Power Pivot, Power BI is accessible enough that all users in an organization can use it to make sense out of all the data at their disposal. Many businesses no longer just rely on data sources locked away on premises but also use cloud-based data solutions (for example, Dynamics 365, Salesforce, Marketo, Google Analytics). These cloud solutions allow users to run their marketing or sales businesses online, and they enable users to get started with a few clicks, without having to set up and maintain servers within their organizations. Cloud solutions contain troves of interesting information relevant for business intelligence, but that information is often not readily accessible to the data warehouse.

Power BI has two main components:

- **PowerBI.com:** This is the main platform that allows users to collaborate on data and create a dashboard (often called a *single pane of glass*) from all the data that's important in a given scenario. Business users can easily sign in to Power BI themselves, with just their corporate email addresses, and then connect to their cloud solutions directly by entering their usernames and passwords. They can then find not just out-of-the-box content from cloud solutions but also content created by their own corporate business intelligence teams or business users. Power BI also allows business users to collaborate with data analysts and traditional BI teams in a seamless and frictionless manner.

- **Power BI Desktop:** Data analysts and authors can use an interactive analytical desktop product called Power BI Desktop. This dedicated report authoring tool enables users to transform data, create powerful reports and visualizations, and easily publish to Power BI. Power BI Desktop is available for free for anyone (**http://ppivot.us/tes3ew**). It contains the same engine that is used for Power Pivot and SQL Server Analysis Services, so most of what you know about Power Pivot can be applied with Power BI Desktop. Where Power Pivot and Power BI Desktop diverge is in how they allow you to visualize the data. Power Pivot is aimed at visualizing in Excel, with traditional PivotTables and PivotCharts, whereas Power BI Desktop has a visualization stack that is aimed at interactive data exploration and more free-form data visualization. To load data, Power BI Desktop uses functionality called Power Query, which allows business users to connect to 100+ data sources and mash up and cleanse data in a very user-friendly manner.

To keep up with the ever-changing industry, Power BI is always moving, and both PowerBI.com and Power BI Desktop are updated every month. This means users get new features and functionality every month of the year. It also means that this book is already outdated even as I am writing it. However, even if some of the tools and techniques covered in this book look slightly different in your version of Power BI, the concepts should still be applicable.

In 2012 the SSAS team released the SSAS tabular model, a version of Power BI Desktop that does not run inside Power BI but runs on a server or as part of Power BI Premium and Azure. The SSAS tabular model is developed using Microsoft Visual Studio. Most of its features and functionality are identical to those in Power BI, but the SSAS tabular model has some additional features that allow for working with larger amounts of data as it is designed for larger-scale enterprise projects.

This book focuses on Power BI, but many of the modeling tips and tricks can be applied to the SSAS tabular model as well. For in-depth information on the tabular model, see *Tabular Modeling in Microsoft SQL Server Analysis Services* by Marco Russo and Alberto Ferrari (**http://ppivot.us/fd3sg4**).

2 - Understanding Dashboards and Reports

In this book, you will learn how to use Power BI to find insights from data. Before you can do that, though, you need to understand some basics. The main goal of building anything in Power BI is to display information from one or several "raw" data sources, either for your own use or to report the information to someone else. When you work with data for yourself, you don't have to think very hard about what it means because it makes sense to you. But when you want to show data to someone else, you have to think a little harder because you need to determine the reasons users are requesting information and what their goals are. You have to think about how to communicate the data so users can easily understand it.

When communicating insights about data, it's important to think about how to *show* and *visualize* the *relevant* information in an *efficient* way. Before you display a bunch of tables and charts, you need to think about why you would use them. You need to consider whether to place one chart adjacent to another chart. Most people don't think about this. This book looks at some examples and investigates how to visualize information in an effective way, following some basic principles.

To determine how to display some particular information, you need to think about the reason someone wants you to show that information. The answer will determine how you shape the data, which you are likely to do in a report. The business intelligence world uses the term *report* to describe a mechanism for sharing information with users. The Bing dictionary tells a similar story for the noun *report*: "an artifact that tells about what happened."

In general, there are three types of reports in business intelligence: dashboards, static reports, and interactive reports. Sometimes you need to use only one type of report, but often the various types work together and even complement each other. Let's look at each type in turn. Then, later in this book, you will be ready to learn how to use Power BI to build dashboards and interactive reports.

Dashboard is a very loaded term in business intelligence that is often seen as being synonymous with BI. People seem to want or think they need dashboards without knowing what they really are or why they need them. But everyone seems to agree that dashboards look sexy and are cool to have. A dashboard can indeed show all the information you need in a consolidated, simple, intuitive, clear, and car-like display.

Unfortunately, dashboards are typically hotspots of flashy charts, traffic lights, and gauges that fail to deliver on the promise of information at a glance. The primary goal of a dashboard should be to deliver the right information in an insightful way. A dashboard should enable someone to spot the information needed at a glance. It's something a user looks at every day or even multiple times a day to see the current rhythm of the business and detect the areas that need immediate attention. Usually a dashboard contains information from multiple areas. For example, it might contain sales, the number of new customers, and employee retention—all in a single pane of glass.

A dashboard should communicate the information the user needs very clearly, at a level that is recognizable and actionable. For example, when a CFO is looking at sales, she probably doesn't need to see the sales for each individual product; she's more likely to want to know whether the organization is on target so that if it's not, she can call the responsible product managers. A product manager probably wants to know which products are on target and which ones are not. Although these two individuals want the same information, they want different levels of detail.

Designing and creating a dashboard is difficult not from a technical standpoint but from a design standpoint. If you ask someone what information he needs, he might tell you "everything." It's your job to distill the information to the right level; a dashboard cannot show *all* the information and should be designed to avoid information overload. You have to be scrupulous about what data you show: You have to pick the most important information in order for a dashboard to stay insightful. This means you need to really get to understand what information the user expects and needs in order for the dashboard to improve his or her day-to-day decision making. Collaborating with your end users is invaluable.

A term often used to describe the information displayed on a dashboard is *key performance indicators* (*KPIs*). Businesses often use KPIs to gauge the success or failure of key metrics in the business. As you create a dashboard, KPIs might give you a good starting point for gathering the right information.

As you think about the design of a dashboard, you need to answer a number of questions:

- How do you position the data?
- Is some information more important than other information?
- How do you visualize the information and then display it effectively?
- How do you use screen real estate as efficiently as possible?
- How do you make the information on the screen actionable so the user can dive deeply in and look at the problems when needed?

A *static report* is the type of report you are probably the most familiar with. Static reports are usually subject oriented, very detailed, and pixel perfect for printing. They try to be exhaustive in terms of information and are meant for users who want to dive deeply into a particular subject. Most companies traditionally have run their businesses using static reports.

Several parameters may be used to generate the data on a static report in different ways. For example, a report may be generated for a particular region or for all regions. A user can often access a static report from a dashboard when he or she wants to drill into more details in a particular area.

Static reports have traditionally been created in Excel or SQL Server Reporting Services, typically by either Excel or BI specialists. As I was writing this book, Power BI announced that it would provide support for uploading Reporting Services reports to Power BI in the near future as well.

> When Power BI adds support for static reports, you will be able to create carefully crafted, pixel perfect reports that are great for long lists of products or customers that can be printed or exported to other formats like Excel or PDF. Users will be able to drill down from a dashboard to interactive reports and also static reports to get all the details that they or the business needs. I do not cover static reports in this book since they have been around a long time and are well documented elsewhere.

Interactive reports give business users a highly visual and dynamic way of looking at data. Instead of showing data in a single static fashion, interactive reports allow users to interact with the data—even on reports created previously—in order to gain insights on the spot. An interactive report allows a user to derive great insights without having to rely on an expert. Whereas a dashboard usually displays data from multiple different subject areas or data sources, an interactive report typically focuses on a single subject area or data source. Static reports are being replaced with interactive reports more and more all the time.

Power BI Tip: Reports vs. Dashboards in Power BI

Power BI allows you to create two different types of reports: interactive reports and dashboards. (As noted earlier, Microsoft plans to provide support for uploading static Reporting Services reports to Power BI, but those reports are not created in Power BI, so I do not show you how to create them in this book.) In Power BI, there is a real difference between interactive reports and dashboards. A *dashboard* is a static single pane of glass that can gather information from many different sources, such as a sales database, CRM and HR systems, and real-time data coming from the factory floor. Dashboards can be created in Power BI based on multiple reports. A Power BI *report*, on the other hand, offers a fully interactive view of the data and may be designed to provide an exhaustive overview of a single subject area. A report in Power BI is also designed to allow interactivity, again to maximize the ability to gain insights without having to change the report itself. It is common for dashboards (containing high-level data) to be backed up by reports (containing detailed data) so that users can drill through from dashboards into reports if they want to know more. This usually also means that reports are created first, and from those reports, the most important data points are selected to create the dashboard.

We will look at creating interactive reports and dashboards in the following chapters of this book. For more information on basic Power BI design concepts, see **http://ppivot.us/hg5sf3**.

Determining What Information to Show

Before you can visualize or report any information, you need to make sure you understand what information you need to show. The creator of a report alone cannot determine what information to show. It's important for the report creator to understand what information the users of the report need in order to improve their insights into the business. This is usually done by interviewing the business users to figure out what they need. To show how this works, this book uses a fictional company, Contoso Communications, and tells the story of an employee named Jim, who is using Power BI to build a solution for his leadership team to use. Prior to this, Jim has never used Power BI, but he has heard that it is similar to working with data in Excel.

Contoso Communications is a telco that sells subscriptions and devices to customers throughout the United States. It is a very traditional company that has been around for 22 years and is mostly focused on traditional sales and services. It has 300 employees in several locations around the United States; most of these employees are in the sales and service departments. Contoso Communications also has a small marketing and product management team. The finance team consists of 5 business analysts, and Jim is a senior business analyst on this team. Contoso mostly outsources IT to external parties, except regarding some of the telco infrastructure. The company uses several systems, including ERP (enterprise resource planning) and CRM (customer relationship management) systems, but it does not have a consolidated data warehouse where it collects all the data.

Contoso Communications has had a difficult year, and the management team feels that it doesn't have a good enough grip on the information in the company. The team often reacts too slowly to changes in the business. The communication business changes rapidly. The members of the management team need to get a better grasp of the overall company numbers, so they can get abreast of the latest information and potentially react better to changes in the market. Jake, the CIO of the company, has been asked to come up with a solution for the management team.

Jim, who reports directly to Jake, has shown in the past that he is very proficient with data and numbers. Jake has asked Jim to come up with a solution to allow the members of the Contoso management team and finance team to easily monitor the financial state of the company, without having to search for relevant information in different places. Jim is unsure what information should be shown, so he sets up time to interview each member of the management team and key members of the financial team and take inventory of their needs.

Jim starts by talking to Jake, who stresses the fact that Contoso Communications depends on several core numbers that are very important to the day-to-day business:

- Overall revenue
- Number of units sold
- Number of devices used
- Number of subscribers
- Number of new customers

In addition to these numbers, the management team wants to compare operational numbers with the targets that the business sets. The management team needs to see short-term numbers so it can react immediately. It needs access to long-term numbers in order to see trends and predict where problems will arise in the future. At Contoso Communications, the fiscal year runs from July 1 to June 30, and the management team expects the information to be represented by fiscal year.

Members of the management team stress that revenue is by far the most important metric, and they want to be able to see the state of revenue for the company over time in order to see overall trends.

Jim also interviews one of his coworkers, Alice, who usually participates in management meetings. He learns that during their most recent meetings, management team members asked Alice to figure out why the company's revenue wasn't growing as much as expected and whether it could be categorized in a certain way. Alice found out that the revenue growth was not equal for all regions; the management team determined that certain regions were underperforming due to marketing issues and was then able to take appropriate action. The management team now wants to keep an active eye on revenue by region to see if the revenue picks up again. The team wants to see the actual revenue compared to the target revenue for the current month and the trend over time.

One of the biggest ongoing efforts in the company during this fiscal year is trying to reduce the cost per unit. The management team wants to be able to see the results of cost reductions for the current period in order to see the results of these efforts.

Jim interviews Bob, the product management director who is responsible for products. Bob tells Jim that one of the things he wants to achieve is to reduce the number of products the company carries in order to save costs. He would like to see an overview of the best- and worst-performing products, by month, for the current fiscal year.

Finally, Jim spends time with Theresa, who runs part of the HR organization. Currently, she says, the sales organization runs all its reports from the HR application, but the reports are limited. Theresa says it would be great if she could show HR data such as the new hire count together with sales information in a single pane of glass that combines all the most important information.

After interviewing the relevant business users, Jim thinks he has enough information to move on. He has figured out what the management team considers to be the most important information, and he can start planning the dashboard and reports he needs to create.

To begin planning his dashboard and reports, Jim creates a list of questions he needs to answer:

- What metrics do I need?
- What values do I need to show the metrics against?
- Where can I find the data needed to display the correct information?

Jim knows that answering these questions won't give him a complete picture, but it will give him some ideas about what data he needs to produce and collect.

Next, he creates an initial inventory of the metrics he needs to collect, based on the interviews he conducted. This is what he comes up with:

- Sum of revenue
- Sum of units
- Sum of usage
- Sum of subscribers
- Sum of revenue target
- Sum of units target
- Sum of usage target
- Sum of subscribers target
- Revenue percentage of total
- Count of potential new customers
- New customer acquisition stage

For each of these metrics, Jim wants to be able to show that number against two other metrics:

- Variance-to-target
- Year-over-year growth, as a percentage

Next, Jim needs to determine what rows and columns to use to show the metrics. He determines that he wants to see the values by:

- Region (country, region, state, city)
- Product
- Time (year, month, fiscal year, fiscal month, current month, past 12 months)

Now that Jim knows what he wants to show in his dashboard and reports, he needs to obtain the correct data.

Jim doesn't have all the data he needs, so he goes over to the IT department to see what it can provide for him. The IT team can give Jim exports from several appropriate systems. This information will appear in an SQL Azure database that the IT team will update every week. The CRM data is not available in that database, but Jim can connect to it directly from Power BI.

Now that Jim has collected enough information and has the data he needs, he can start building the dashboard and reports. Chapter 3 describes how Jim collects some of the data he needs to build a detailed report, and Chapter 6 describes how he assembles it into a dashboard.

3 - Collecting and Preparing the Data

This chapter describes how Jim collects the data needed for the Contoso sales report by importing data from his data source. It also shows how he downloads and uses Power BI Desktop to prepare and optimize that data for analytics and visualization.

If you would like to follow along with Jim's example as you read the book, you can download the sample file from **http://ppivot.us/file34ss**. The sample already has the data imported, so you don't need to worry about working through the data import part of the example; instead, you can begin working through the example starting from Figure 3.33, where we import all the data and start working with the model. If you would rather have the already finished file, you can download it from **http://ppivot.us/sampl32d**.

Installing Power BI Desktop

Jim needs to show the first version of the dashboard to his manager in a few days. Jim is very proficient with Excel and Power Pivot, and even though Power BI Desktop is a different product, Jim's current skills will enable him to use Power BI Desktop without requiring too much new learning.

Jim goes to **http://www.PowerBI.com** and selects Power BI Desktop under the Products menu.

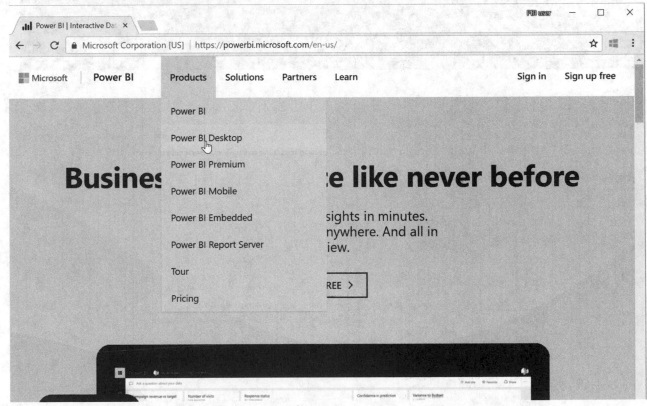

Figure 3.1: Selecting Power BI Desktop from the landing page.

The Power BI Desktop page opens, and Jim can select Download to download Power BI Desktop for free.

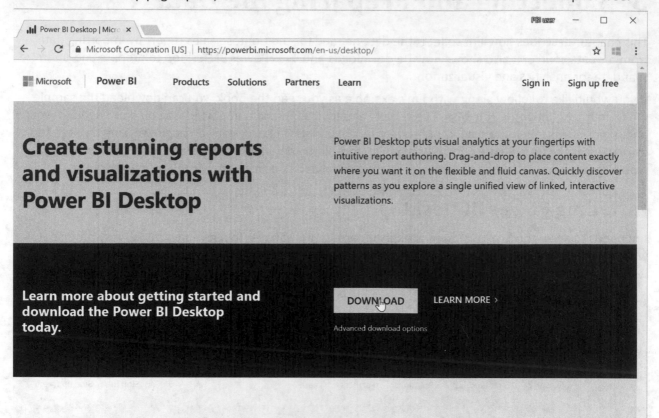

Figure 3.2: Downloading Power BI Desktop.

After Power BI Desktop is downloaded, Jim double-clicks the download to start the installer.

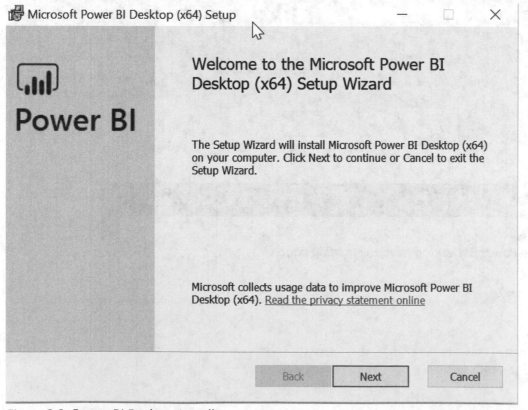

Figure 3.3: Power BI Desktop installer.

Power BI Desktop Tip: Choosing a Version

Power BI Desktop is available in two versions: 32 bit and 64 bit. The difference between the two has to do with the amount of memory Power BI Desktop can use on your machine. When you install Power BI Desktop, the installer automatically determines what version it can install, and it chooses the 64-bit version by default. You can, however, manually choose a version at **http://ppivot.us/khg23s**. Or, if you choose to install Power BI Desktop from the Microsoft Store, you automatically get updates every month, as soon as they are available.

If possible, choose the 64-bit version, which allows you to work with larger amounts of data. Not everyone has this luxury, though, as an IT department may centrally roll out the 32-bit version of Power BI Desktop for the entire organization. Even though I prefer the 64-bit version, having the 32-bit version won't prohibit you from working with Power BI Desktop.

When Power BI Desktop is installed, Jim opens it to start his work.

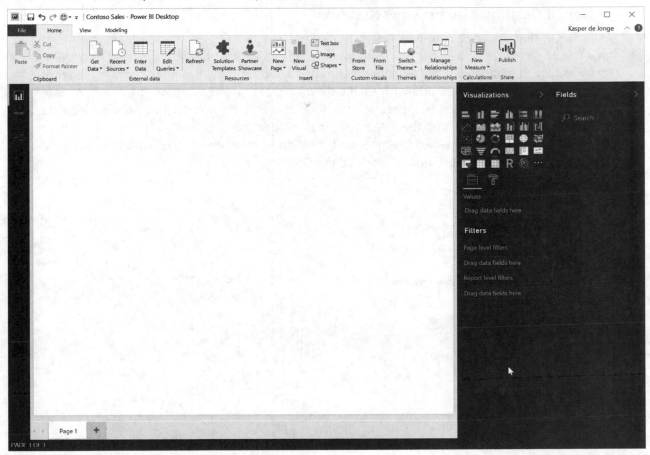

Figure 3.4: A new Power BI Desktop file.

Power BI Desktop Tip: Power BI Desktop vs. Excel

Working with Power BI Desktop is very different from working with Excel. Some differences are immediately visible, such as Power BI having no grid and having a pane open on the right.

Whereas in Excel you add charts directly to a worksheet, with Power BI Desktop you use a freeform canvas that doesn't have the restriction of gridlines. (No more messing up alignment because you inserted a new row!) You start creating a new visualization by selecting a field from the Fields pane; Power BI adds the field to the field well and adds a visualization in the first available free spot on the main canvas. You can later drag the visualization to anyplace on the freeform canvas.

Another difference between Power BI and Excel is that the Power BI canvas is limited to one screen, and you cannot scroll outside it. The main canvas uses a default aspect ratio of 16:9, but you can change it to 4:3.

In Power BI, it is also possible to add filters to all the visualizations on a worksheet by adding a filter to the Filters pane. This pane consists of several sections:

- **Visual Level Filters:** This area shows up only when you select a visual on the canvas. Any filters added here will filter just the visual.

- **Page Level Filters:** Filters added here will filter everything on the current page.

- **Drillthrough Filters:** Filters placed here will allow this page to be used in a drillthrough filter. (You'll learn more about this later.)

- **Report Level Filters:** This area is for filters that filter every page created in the current Power BI Desktop file.

Despite these and quite a number of other differences between Excel and Power BI, you will find that transitioning from Excel to Power BI is not difficult.

Power BI Desktop Tip: Preview Features

As noted earlier, PowerBI.com and Power BI Desktop are updated every month, which means new features constantly become available. Many of these features are first available as preview features, which means you can use them before they become fully available features. Most of the time small changes are made with each new update of Power BI, and often you can update Power BI without any issues. However, Microsoft reserves the right to change preview features and doesn't provide support on these features, so if you use them, you do so at your own risk. To turn on preview features—which I recommend you do to familiarize yourself with the upcoming features—simply select File, Options and Settings, Options.

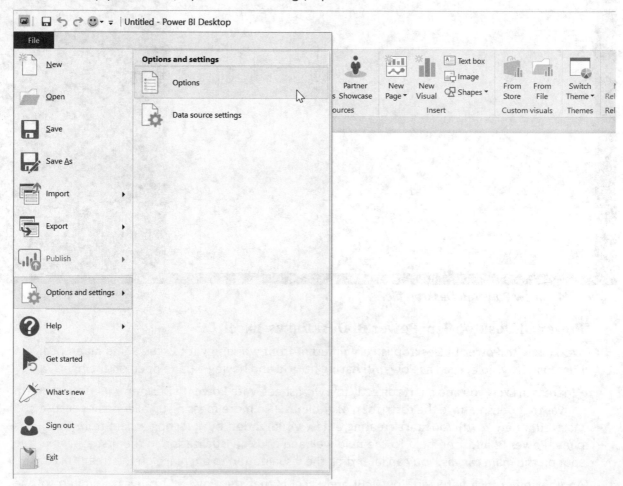

Figure 3.5: Turning on the preview features.

You can then select the preview features you want to turn on. Figure 3.6 shows the preview features available to me at the time of this writing, though I expect that you will have very different preview features available.

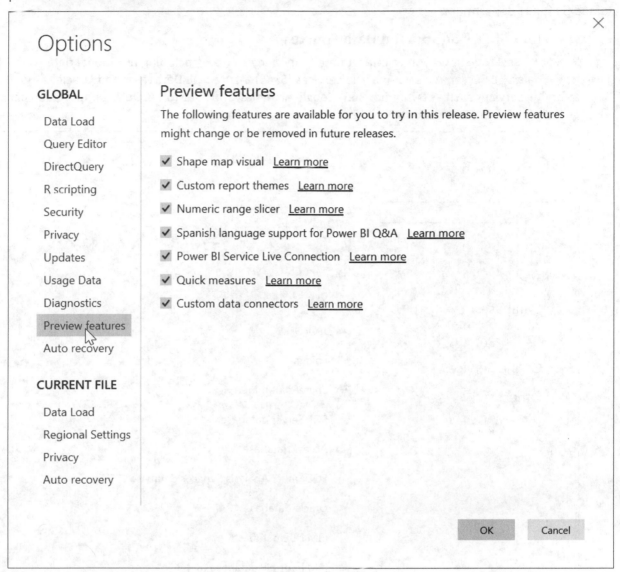

Figure 3.6: Selecting preview features.

Importing Data

The information Jim wants to use for his report is stored in an Azure SQL Database that is set up and maintained by the IT department.

Data Model Tip: Supported Data Sources

Power BI Desktop allows you to import data from many sources, including traditional data sources such as SQL Server, Access, Analysis Services (SSAS), Azure SQL Database, and Oracle, as well as online services such as Dynamics 365, Google Analytics, and Salesforce. During import, you can choose from a large set of data sources.

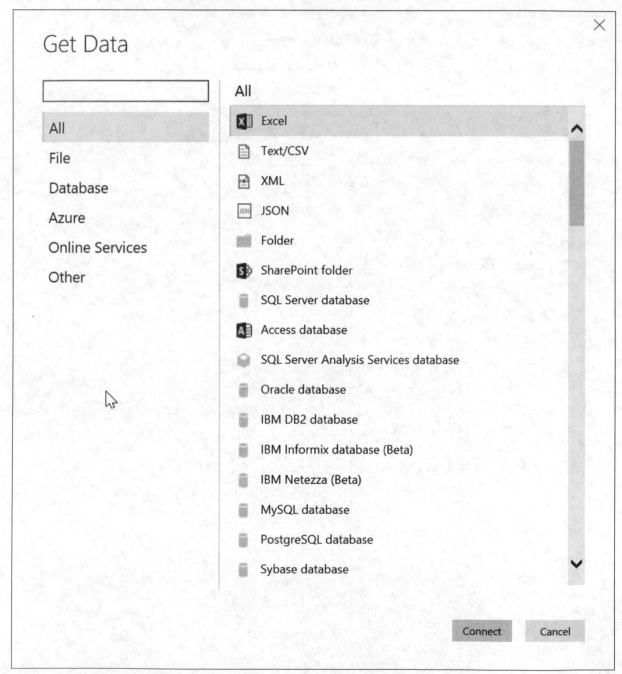

Figure 3.7: Some of the data sources available in Power BI Desktop.

Jim needs to get his data from the Azure SQL Database, so he clicks Get Data on the Power BI Desktop Home ribbon and then clicks More.

Figure 3.8: Selecting more data sources.

In the Get Data dialog, Jim selects Azure SQL Database as the type of data source he wants to connect to. Then he clicks Connect.

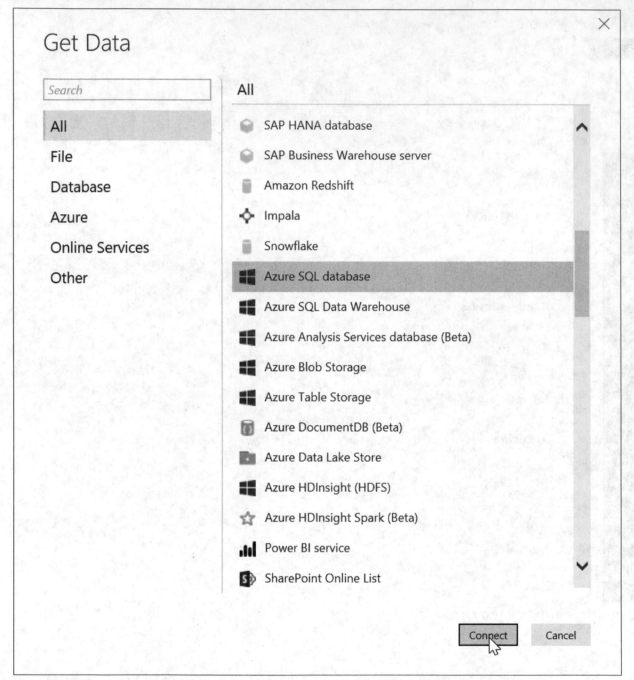

Figure 3.9: Get Data dialog.

In the next step of the import process, Jim chooses how to connect to the data source.

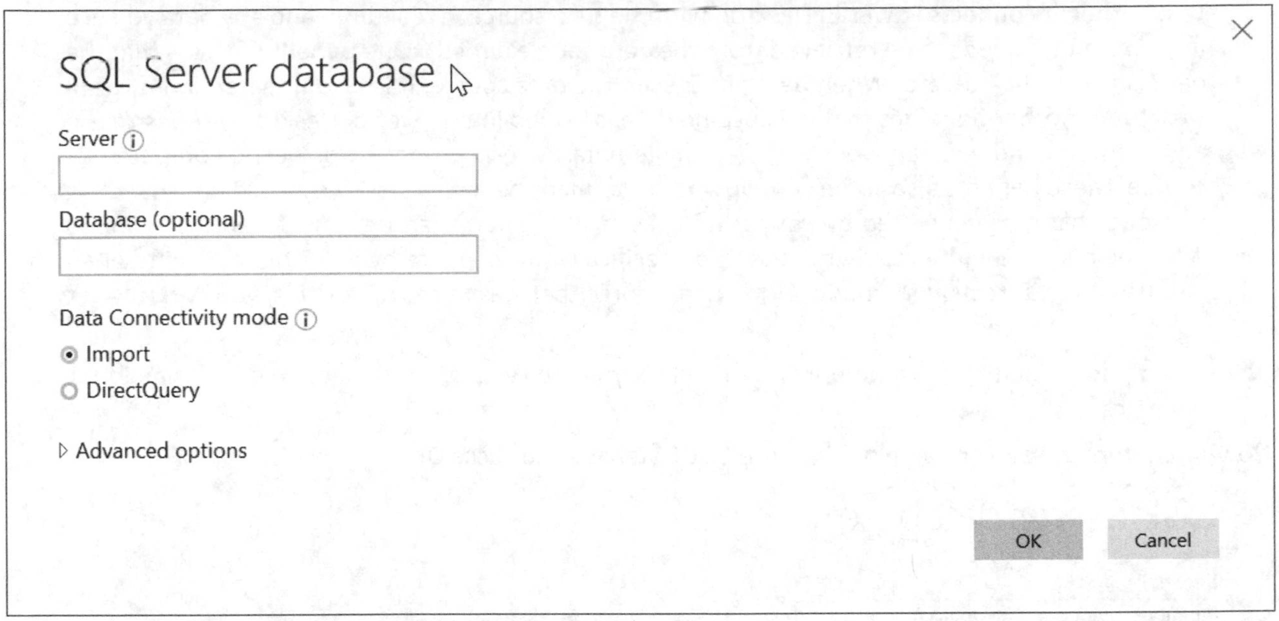

Figure 3.10: Connecting to the data source.

Data Model Tip: Import vs. DirectQuery

When connecting to a data source, you can often choose the connectivity mode. In most cases, the mode can be either Import or DirectQuery, though some data sources support only Import mode. Choosing the mode is a very important step as the two modes are fundamentally different, and the mode cannot be changed at a later stage.

Import mode loads the data from the data source into the Power BI analytical engine. This special analytical engine, called VertiPaq, loads the data into the memory of your computer, which means the data can be analyzed at the speed of thought.

To allow for a large amount of data to be analyzed on your computer, VertiPaq compresses the data by storing the duplicate values from each column only once in memory and replacing each original value with a small number that points to the real value, which is stored somewhere else in memory. Figure 3.11 shows which values will be replaced with a single pointer; the colors indicate which values are compressed in memory by replacing the value with a small numerical pointer value.

ID	Year	Month	SalesPerson	Value
1	2010	January	Jeff	34
2	2010	January	Marty	54
3	2010	February	Jeff	554
4	2010	February	James	23

Figure 3.11: Visualizing compression in the data model.

Compression is especially helpful when there are many duplicate values in the columns. Thanks to compression, large amounts of data can be loaded into a small amount of memory; you can even achieve tenfold compression rates. Thanks to this compression, for data loaded into Power BI, there is not a limit on the number of rows you can import. (Of course, though, if your computer runs out of memory, it cannot read more data.) When data changes in the data source, it is not automatically and immediately reflected in Power BI Desktop. To update the data, you can refresh the data, which causes the data to be loaded into Power BI Desktop again.

DirectQuery mode is different from Import mode as it doesn't load the data into Power BI Desktop. Rather, it connects Power BI Desktop with the data source in real time, and any data you use in your reports needs to be retrieved from the data source directly. One benefit of this is that the data is always up-to-date: When data changes in the data source, it is also updated in Power BI Desktop. Another benefit is that because no data is loaded into Power BI Desktop, it doesn't use any memory, and you can work with very large datasets using a not-so-powerful computer. Of course, these benefits also come with downsides as many data sources have a hard time handling the load that gets generated by Power BI Desktop, and reports can be slow. DirectQuery mode often works best with data sources set up specifically for analytics by an IT department; when you try to use DirectQuery mode with a data source that wasn't set up for this, you typically get poor performance.

It is a good idea to choose Import mode unless you are certain the data source is designed for analytics.

Now Jim enters the server name of his Azure SQL Database and clicks OK.

SQL Server database

Server ⓘ

jlu8lk81kx.database.windows.net

Database (optional)

Data Connectivity mode ⓘ
- ⦿ Import
- ◯ DirectQuery

▷ Advanced options

OK   Cancel

Figure 3.12: Entering the server name.

Jim needs to enter the credentials the IT department created for him, so he selects Database and enters his username and password and clicks Connect.

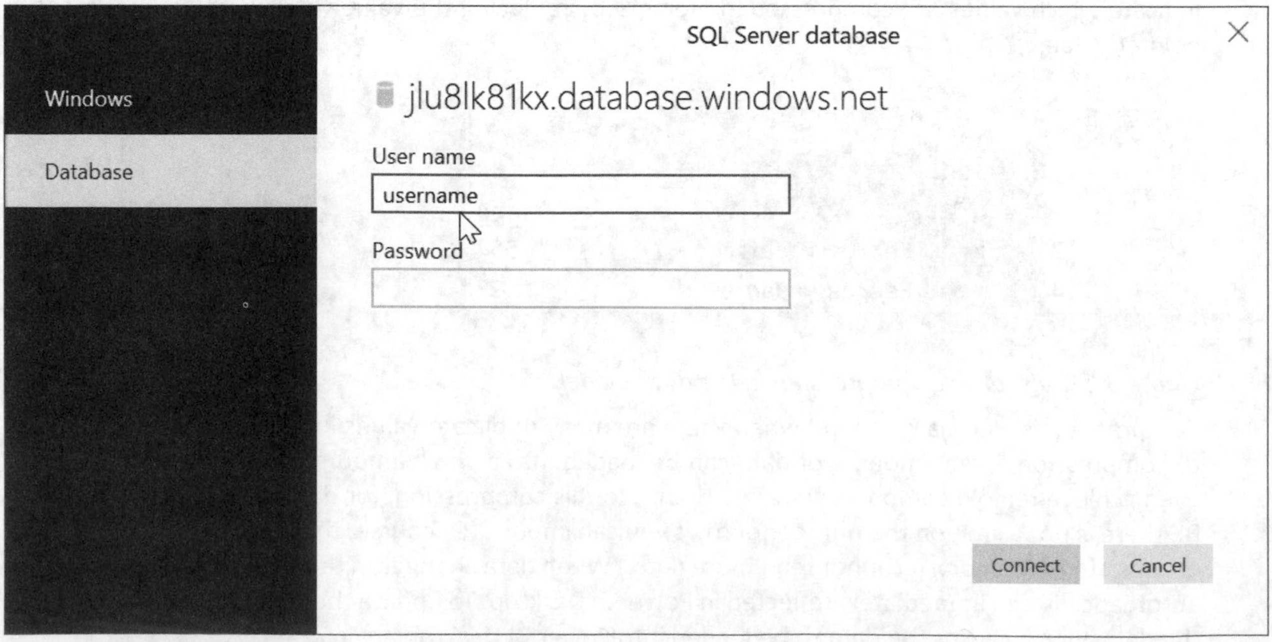

SQL Server database   ✕

Windows

Database

🖳 jlu8lk81kx.database.windows.net

User name

username

Password

Connect   Cancel

Figure 3.13: Entering database credentials.

When he is connected to the database server, Jim can select the database he wants to use for his reports. In this case, the database is ContosoSales, so he expands its node and selects all the tables in this database.

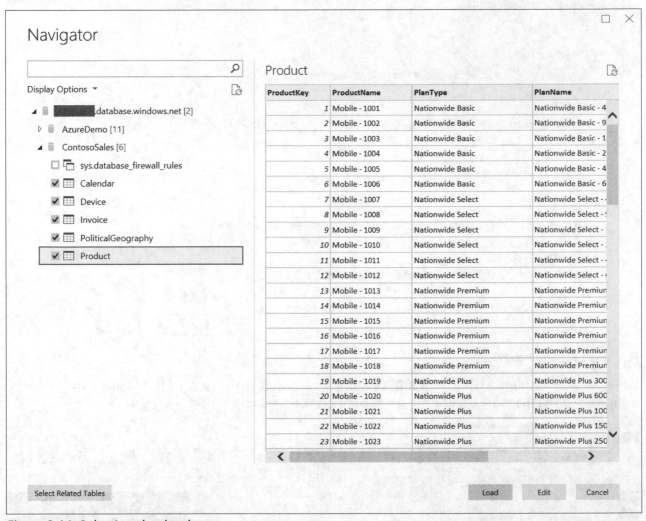

Figure 3.14: Selecting the database.

Data Model Tip: Editing a Query

Instead of loading data directly, you can make changes to data by using the Power BI Query Editor. The Power BI Query Editor is based on a product called Power Query, another product that found its way into the Excel Get Data experience with Excel 2016. It is built and designed to transform any type of raw data into tables that can then be used to build the data model. The Power Query engine allows Power BI to connect to a large number of different data sources, and it is also used to transform and clean raw data. The Power Query Editor has a simple UI that allows business users to make transformations that used to be really difficult—for example, unpivoting data with just a click instead of working through multiple steps. The Power Query Editor also allows other simple transformations, such as renaming columns, changing case, replacing values, and splitting columns.

Any change made to a table creates a step in the Power Query Editor in Power BI. You can use these steps to quickly move between the changes made. Under the covers, Power BI generates a script using the M language. (I don't cover Power Query and the M language in detail in this book, but you can find more information in the great books *M Is for (Data) Monkey: A Guide to the M Language in Excel Power Query* by Ken Puls and Miguel Escobar, at **http://ppivot.us/iuyfd4e**, and *Power Query for Power BI and Excel* by Chris Webb, at **http://ppivot.us/nvdsf3s**.)

Now that the data is selected, Jim clicks Load to load all the data into Power BI Desktop, and the date begins loading.

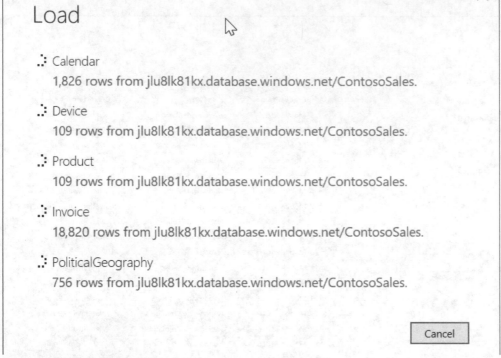

Load

⠿ Calendar

1,826 rows from jlu8lk81kx.database.windows.net/ContosoSales.

⠿ Device

109 rows from jlu8lk81kx.database.windows.net/ContosoSales.

⠿ Product

109 rows from jlu8lk81kx.database.windows.net/ContosoSales.

⠿ Invoice

18,820 rows from jlu8lk81kx.database.windows.net/ContosoSales.

⠿ PoliticalGeography

756 rows from jlu8lk81kx.database.windows.net/ContosoSales.

Cancel

Figure 3.15: Loading data.

When all the data is loaded into Power BI Desktop, Jim can start analyzing it. All the columns and tables from the SQL database are available in the Power BI Fields pane on the right.

Figure 3.16: Data loaded and ready to be analyzed.

Jim selects RevenueAmount from the Invoice table and DeviceName from the Device table, and Power BI Desktop automatically creates a visual that shows the sum of RevenueAmount by DeviceName.

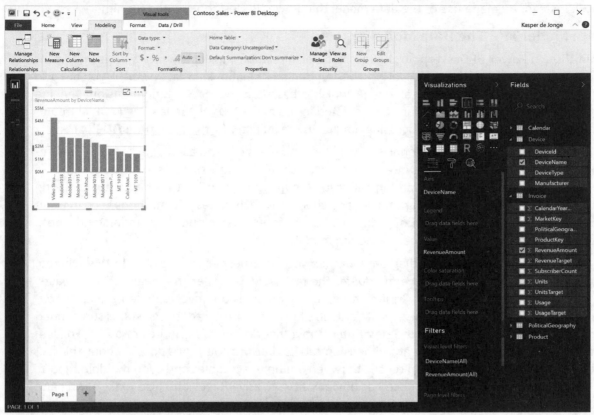

Figure 3.17: Data visualized in Power BI.

Data Model Tip: Data Types

Every column in Power BI Desktop is strongly typed. This means each column has a defined type, such as number or text. Whenever possible, Power BI Desktop retrieves the data type from the data source. For example, SQL Server provides this information, but when it is unavailable, Power BI Desktop tries to determine the data type through detection. Many operations are directly based on this data type. For example, when Jim clicked the RevenueAmount column, Power BI Desktop recognized that this is a numeric data type and automatically aggregated the values by using SUM.

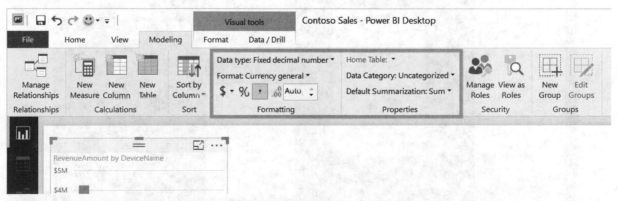

Figure 3.18: The data type is shown in the Modeling tab.

All values in a column must be of the same type in order to be stored inside the data model. If they are not all the same type, Power BI Desktop will throw an error because some operations are not possible when data in a column is not the right type; for example, you cannot do a SUM operation on a text column. You can change the data type manually when needed.

When creating the visual in Figure 3.17, Jim combined data from different tables without much effort. He didn't have to use VLOOKUP to consolidate all the data into one worksheet first, as he would have had to do in Excel. Instead, he made use of the data model that Power BI Desktop created for him.

Data Model Tip: The Data Model

Even though Power BI Desktop automatically detects relationships in the model, it is important to understand how relationships work. To best understand relationships in Power BI, you need to look at the history of its analytical engine, which is based on the SSAS multidimensional engine (**http://ppivot.us/DBRLO**). This product, created in the mid-1990s, is the leading MOLAP (multi-dimensional online analytical processing) engine in the industry (**http://ppivot.us/IDCXA**).

SSAS has for years served traditional BI developers and users of Excel as the backend for their reports. These traditional business intelligence projects tend to use a star or snowflake schema—a design approach favored by Ralph Kimball (**http://ppivot.us/MPMZP**) that has become the de facto design standard for data warehouses and cubes. The techniques and methods used in traditional data warehousing shine through in Power BI. A Power BI developer who understands these techniques can more easily create and design models.

In the star schema, the model diagram looks (as you would expect) like a star. In this schema, the center of the star is called the *fact table*. The fact table describes the measurements, facts, or metrics of a business process. In Jim's case, the fact table is the Invoice table because it contains the invoices that are the metrics of Contoso's business. The center of the star is surrounded by dimensions. Each *dimension* is a descriptive table that describes attributes of a fact. For Jim, Product and PoliticalGeography are dimension tables that provide more details about the fact table. Dimension tables are often reused between multiple fact tables and even multiple reports or cubes. Storing the data only once has obvious storage advantages and also make slicing and dicing of data easier for the end user of the report.

Figure 3.19 shows Jim's tables rearranged into a star shape, with the Invoice table in the middle and the other tables around it. This arrangement is based on the keys inside the tables; for example, the Invoice table contains ProductKey, and the Product table also contains ProductKey. ProductKey in the Invoice table is called a *foreign key*, and ProductKey in the Product table is a *primary key*. One single unique product has many different invoices for the same product. This is a one-to-many relationship, and it is the most common type of relationship.

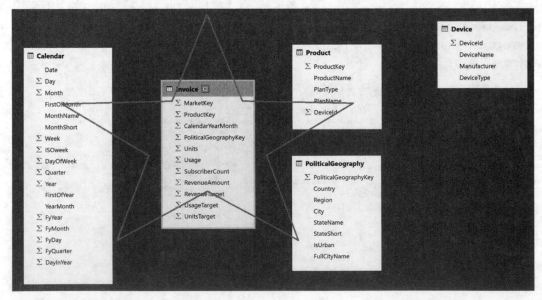

Figure 3.19: The star shape in the schema.

As you can see, there is an outlier in this diagram: the Device table. This table is an outlier because it has no relationship with the Invoice table at the center of the star; however, it is related to the Product table. Because of this outlier, this diagram is actually a snowflake rather than a star.

Jim wants to extend his visual to add a new slicer that allows him to select a year. He therefore drags in Year from the Calendar table and selects the slicer visual.

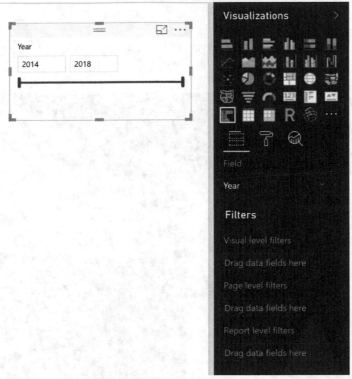

Figure 3.20: Adding the year as a slicer.

Power BI Tip: Slicers

Slicers, which became famous in Excel 2010, offer a powerful way of filtering reports in Power BI. A slicer shows a list of values as part of the report, and when the values are selected, the slicer filters (or slices) the report based on the selected values.

Jim expects that when he changes the value of the slicer, the RevenueAmount by DeviceName visual will change to reflect the data for the selected years. However, when he changes the value of the slicer, nothing happens.

To see if something is wrong with the model, Jim switches to the relationships view by clicking on the relationships icon on the left of the Power BI Desktop window.

Figure 3.21: The relationships icon opens the relationships view.

When the relationships view of the Power BI Desktop model opens, Jim can see the tables, their fields, and the relationships between tables. It's pretty obvious in the diagram shown in Figure 3.22 that the columns between Invoice and Calendar are not related.

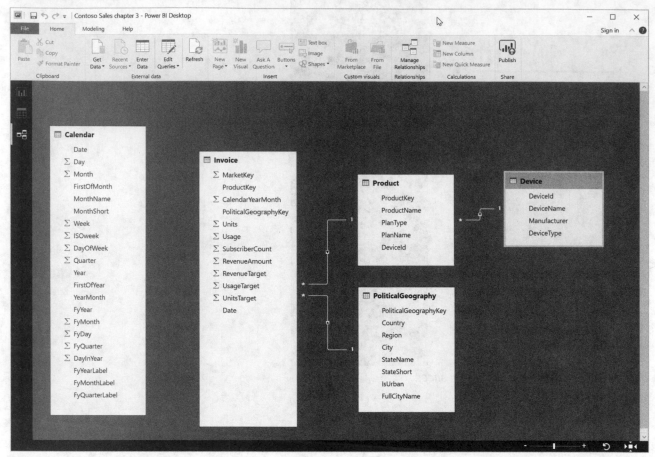

Figure 3.22: Power BI Desktop relationships view.

Jim tries to create the relationships by dragging and dropping between the Invoice table's CalendarYear-Month column and the Calendar table's YearMonth column, but he gets an error.

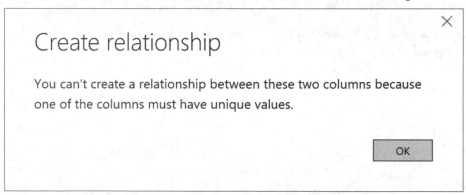

Figure 3.23: Power BI Desktop cannot create the relationship.

The relationship Jim has tried to create here is not a one-to-many relationship because the values of the Calendar table's YearMonth column are not unique; they need to be in a one-to-many relationship where the column from the dimension table is a primary key. To be able to create this relationship, Jim needs to find two columns between the two tables that allow him to create this relationship: He needs a primary key from the dimension table and a foreign key from the fact table. For example, between Invoice[Product-Key] and Product[ProductKey], there is only a unique ProductKey in the Product table (the primary key), but there are many occurrences of the same ProductKey in the invoice table—one for each invoice. (Here ProductKey is the foreign key.)

Jim uses the data view in Power BI Desktop to look at all the data in the tables.

MarketKey	ProductKey	CalendarYearMonth	PoliticalGeographyKey	Units	Usage	Sub
467	22	201701		67	450	384.75
633	11	201706		33	450	384.75
335	27	201702		35	450	384.75
71	71	201702		71	450	384.75
461	1	201709		461	450	384.75
679	106	201709		79	450	384.75
695	57	201702		95	450	384.75

Figure 3.24: Using the Power BI Desktop data view.

He starts by looking at the Date column from the Invoice table. Jim notices that the Date column in the Invoice table does not contain data on the day level but only has values for each month of the year. Because this is the only Date column in the Invoice table, Jim needs to use this column to create the relationship to the Calendar table.

Jim looks at the columns in the DateTable table. He needs to find the primary key—that is, the column that contains unique values for each row in the table. He finds that the Date column is the only column that will work in this case.

In order for Jim to create a relationship between the Invoice and Calendar tables, the values from the two columns need to be identical. Jim can't change the Date column from the Calendar table to get rid of the date part of the value because doing so would make this value no longer unique for each row in the table. To create the relationship, Jim must create a field of the date data type in the Invoice table by adding a day part to the CalendarYearMonth column of the DateTable table. In Excel, he could easily achieve this by creating a formula. Although it is not possible to directly use Excel formulas in Power BI Desktop, it is possible to use the Power BI Desktop Query Editor to get the same results.

Jim knows he can change the tables by changing the query, so he selects Edit Queries in the Power BI Desktop Home tab.

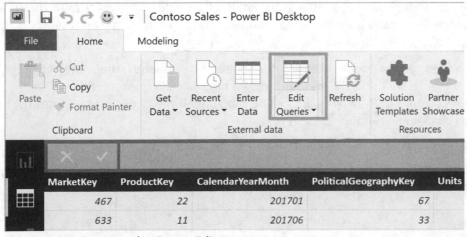

Figure 3.25: Opening the Query Editor.

In the Query Editor, Jim selects the CalendarYearMonth column to transform it into a date.

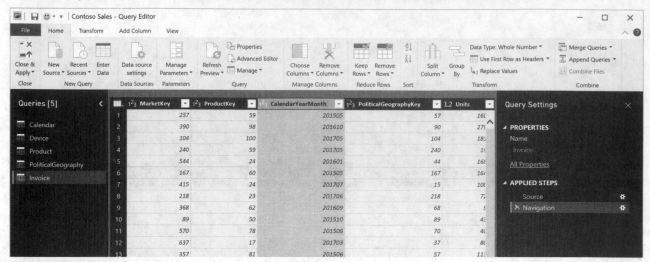

Figure 3.26: Selecting the column in the Query Editor.

Currently the column contains only years and months, but by adding a day to it, Jim can make it into a date. He doesn't have an actual invoice day, but he can choose the first day of the month to change the column to a date column. Jim can use the Query Editor to transform the data in this way. He starts by adding a new column to the table by clicking Custom Column on the Add Column tab.

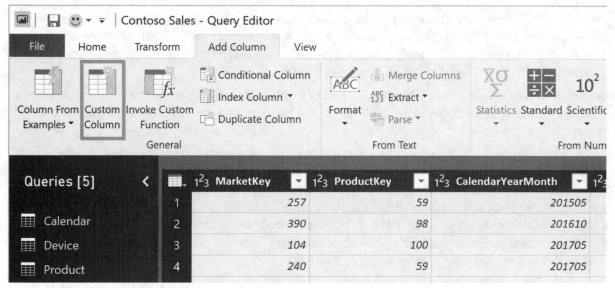

Figure 3.27: Adding a new custom column.

In the dialog that appears, Jim can add an expression that gives him the date value. Jim first tries to create an expression that simply appends 01, for the first day of the month, to the CalendarYearMonth value:

```
=[CalendarYearMonth] & "01"
```

This does not give him the expected values. It looks like the 01 is added to the CalendarYearMonth value instead of being appended to the end. Jim understands that the data type is again important here: If he changes the CalendarYearMonth column to the text data type, he can append the two values. He uses the `Number.ToText` function to change the number column to text:

```
=Number.ToText([CalendarYearMonth]) & "01"
```

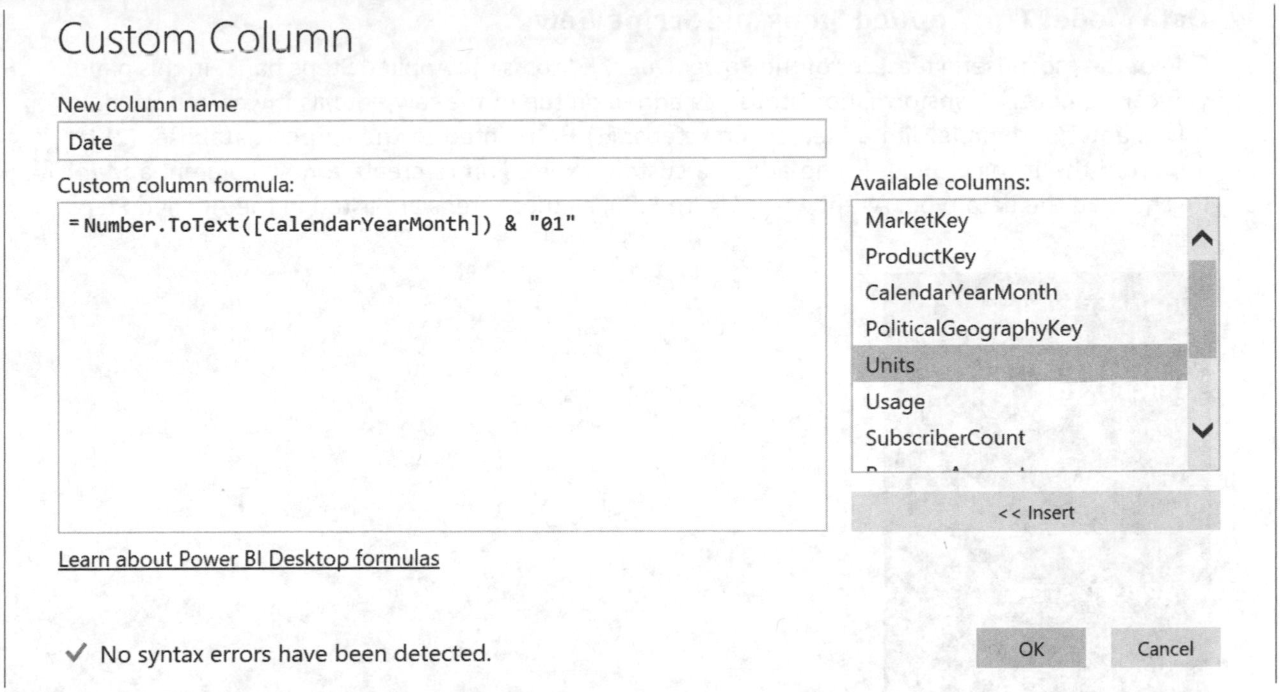

Custom Column

New column name

Date

Custom column formula:

= Number.ToText([CalendarYearMonth]) & "01"

Available columns:

MarketKey
ProductKey
CalendarYearMonth
PoliticalGeographyKey
Units
Usage
SubscriberCount

<< Insert

Learn about Power BI Desktop formulas

✔ No syntax errors have been detected.

OK   Cancel

Figure 3.28: Using Power BI Desktop formulas.

Data Model Tip: Query Editor Formulas

The formula Jim just added here provides an example of using the M language, mentioned earlier. Most of the time you don't need to actually type in a formula because the UI is very capable of doing most of this work for you. But there are many things M can do, and learning some M language will open many doors. For more information, you can find the full M reference document at **http://ppivot.us/m3rsgs**.

This gives Jim the expected values. However, although they look like the right values, they are not in a typical date format; they appear in YYYYMMDD format rather than the MM/DD/YYYY format that Jim expected to see.

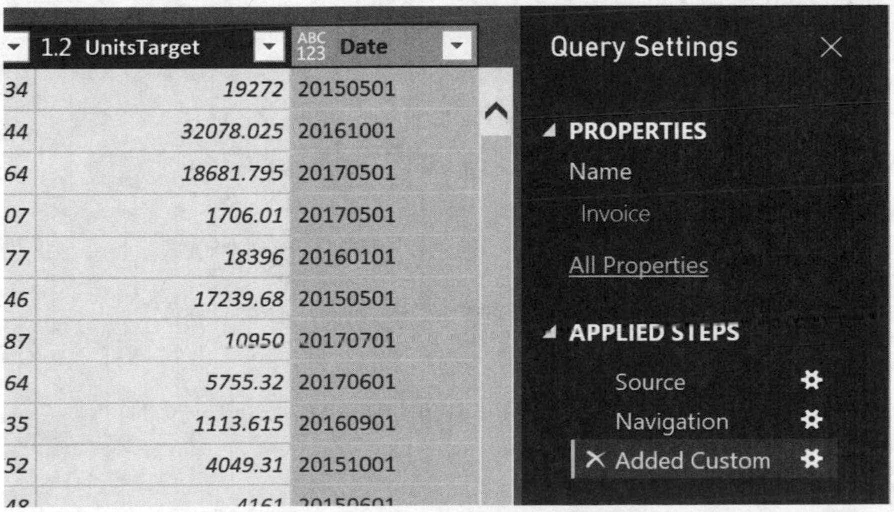

1.2 UnitsTarget	ABC 123 Date	Query Settings ✕
34	19272	20150501
44	32078.025	20161001
64	18681.795	20170501
07	1706.01	20170501
77	18396	20160101
46	17239.68	20150501
87	10950	20170701
64	5755.32	20170601
35	1113.615	20160901
52	4049.31	20151001
48	4161	20150601

Query Settings ✕

▲ PROPERTIES

Name

Invoice

All Properties

▲ APPLIED STEPS

Source   ✿

Navigation   ✿

✕ Added Custom ✿

Figure 3.29: Adding a new column with date values.

Jim checks the data type on the Transform tab and sees that it is still set to Any, so he changes it to Date, and this causes the dates to really look like dates; for example, he now sees 5/1/2015 rather than 20150501.

Data Model Tip: Applied Steps and Script View

One of the most useful features of the Power Query Editor is the Applied Steps pane. In this pane, you can see every transformation steps you added on top of the raw data as it was imported. In this chapter's example, Jim added several steps: (1) He pointed to the source database, (2) he imported the Invoice table, (3) he added a custom expression to create a new column, and (4) he changed the data type. As shown in Figure 3.30, all these steps are listed in the Applied Steps pane.

Figure 3.30: All the custom steps added to the Invoice table.

A very useful feature in the Power Query Editor is that you can go back to any step in the process and make changes or even delete steps and insert other steps. Thanks to the Applied Steps pane, you will never lose the transformations you have made.

The Power Query Editor has an even more powerful option, called script view. As mentioned earlier, all transformations together generate a script. You have full access to this script: Simply go to the View tab and click Advanced Editor.

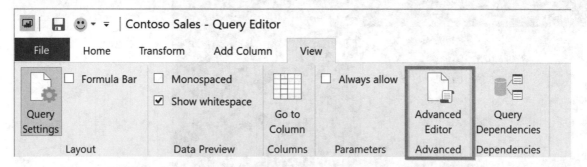

Figure 3.31: Opening the Advanced Editor.

When the Advanced Editor is open, you have full access to the script that was generated. (This is sometimes useful in more advanced scenarios.)

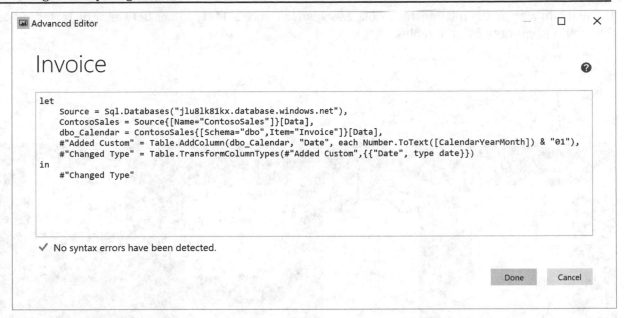

Figure 3.32: Viewing a script in the Advanced Editor.

Notice that the same steps are available in the script as in the Applied Steps pane. If you make changes to a script and apply the changes, they will be reflected in the Applied Steps pane.

To apply the changes to his model, Jim needs to click Close & Apply on the Home tab.

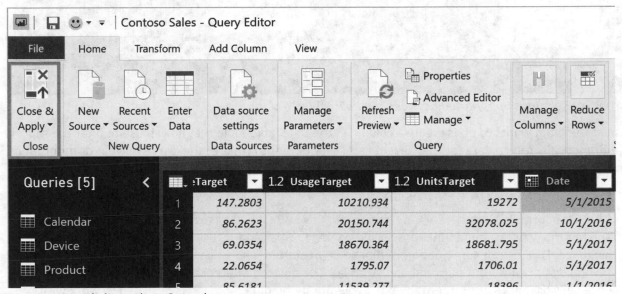

Figure 3.33: Clicking Close & Apply.

When the query changes are applied to the model, Jim has a column that contains dates that he can use to create a relationship to the Calendar table.

Jim opens the diagram view again to create a relationship between the Invoice and Calendar tables. He selects the newly created Date field from the Invoice table and drags it to the Date field of the DateTable table to create the relationship between the two tables.

The diagram with all the relationships looks as shown in Figure 3.34. The lines between the tables indicate the relationships between the tables.

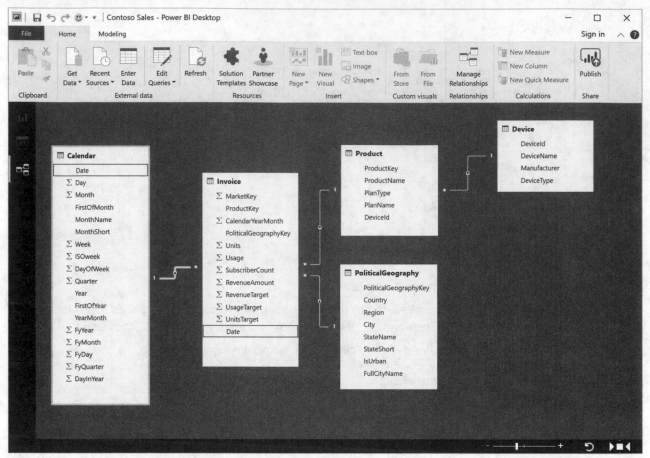

Figure 3.34: Relationships created between multiple tables.

The next thing Jim wants to do is create a column in the DateTable table that he can use to filter the report and automatically return data for the current fiscal year or month (that is, the last fiscal year or month for which he has invoices).

Data Model Tip: DAX Expressions

DAX is the formula language for data loaded into Power BI. It looks like the Excel formula language and has many of the same functions, including `DATE`, `SUM`, and `LEFT`. Also like the Excel formula language, DAX uses a combination of functions, operators, and values in its formulas. But it has several distinct differences from Excel formulas. The biggest difference is that DAX doesn't reference cells or ranges but rather tables and columns in the data model. It is designed to work with relational data and to achieve very fast dynamic aggregations that utilize the highly optimized in-memory engine. DAX is designed for speed: It can quickly look up and calculate values across very large columns or tables.

There are two types of DAX expressions:

- **Calculated columns or tables:** These expressions enrich the model. A calculated column, which is based on a DAX formula, is a new column added to a table. The DAX formula will be executed for each and every row inside the table, and the results of the formula will be stored in the table together with the values that came in during the import. A calculated table is similar except that you can use a calculated table and a DAX expression to create an entire table. When you use a calculated column or table in a report, the columns look and feel as though they were imported into the model together with the rest of the columns of the table.

- **Measures:** Measures are DAX expressions that you use in analysis when aggregating values of a column against a row or column. For example, for Jim to do a sum of revenue that he wants to pivot by year or by products, he would need to create an aggregation of the Revenue column from the Invoice table as a measure and use that in a matrix. The measure will be calculated for that matrix, and the results will be calculated on the fly.

We'll look at many examples of both types of DAX expressions throughout this book.

Data Model Tip: DAX vs. M

As you might have gathered by now, Power BI Desktop is a marriage of a couple different products: Power Pivot, Power Query, and Power View. While Power Pivot and Power Query are designed for different tasks, they do have some overlap. Like Power Query, Power Pivot allows for some transformations, but there are some fundamental differences. Power Query is used to import data into Power BI, and the M formulas, under the covers, transform the raw data into the shape that you want for the table. Power Query is also very smart: It tries to fold transformations directly to the data source—and this means the data source, not Power BI, will handle the transformation. In the end, every query in Power Query results in a single table. With DAX, you can only work with data that has already been imported into the model, so DAX only allows you to shape the data that is already loaded into the model. As you have already seen, DAX can be used in two ways—to enrich data and for analysis. In general, the recommendation is to use Power Query for importing and transforming data and to use DAX for calculations. In this chapter you have already seen an example of transforming data when adding a date column, and you will see a DAX transformation next.

Jim needs to create a new column that compares all the dates in the DateTable table to the last fiscal date for which he has an invoice; the column should return 1 if the month and year in the Calendar table are the same as the last fiscal year or month. The Calendar table contains two different dates: calendar and fiscal dates. Because the fiscal year runs from July 1 to June 30 at Contoso Communications, when the calendar date is 11/30/2018, Contoso's fiscal date is 5/31/2019.

In order to determine the last month for which he has data, Jim needs to find the last invoice date. He decides to create a measure to get this date so that he can reuse that value in other places.

Jim wants to use the Date column in the Invoice table, but that would return the actual date, not the fiscal date. In order to get the last fiscal date for each invoice, Jim can leverage the information in the Calendar table. He can use the DAX `RELATED` function to look up the fiscal date information from the Calendar table for each invoice date by using the table relationship. In the Fields pane, Jim right-clicks on the Calendar table and clicks New Column.

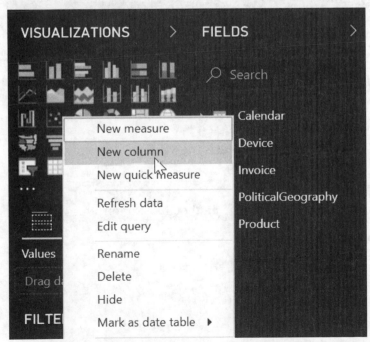

Figure 3.35: Adding a new calculated column to the model.

Jim uses the following expression:

```
Fiscal Date = DATE(
                   RELATED(Calendar[FyYear])
                   ,RELATED(Calendar[FyMonth])
                   ,1
                   )
```

> This formula uses the DATE function to create a date value in the Invoice table. The DATE function expects three arguments: a year, a month, and a day. Jim uses the RELATED function to get the FyYear and FyMonth values from the DateTable table. The RELATED function then uses the relationship between the tables to get the values from the DateTable table for each row in the Invoice table.

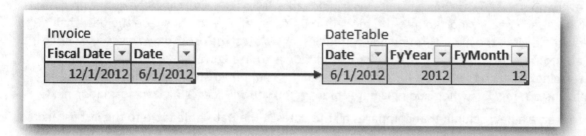

Figure 3.36: The RELATED function uses the relationship between tables to get values from the other table.

Because Jim is using data from a different table in the model, he must use a DAX formula here instead of doing this in the Query Editor.

This expression adds the FiscalDate calculated column to the table.

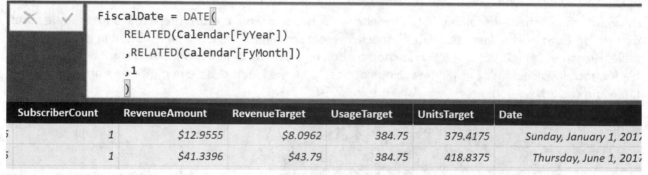

Figure 3.37: The values from the calculated column are added for each row.

The data type of the newly created FiscalDate column is set to Date/Time, but the time part isn't needed, so Jim changes it to just Date in the Modeling tab.

To create a measure to select the fiscal date of the last invoice, Jim selects the Modeling tab and clicks New Measure.

> Measures and calculated columns can be added in two ways: through the Modeling tab or by right-clicking on the Fields pane. I personally use the Fields pane method most often.

He enters the following formula in the formula bar:

```
[Absolute Last Invoice Fiscal Date]=
        LASTDATE(Invoice[Fiscal Date])
```

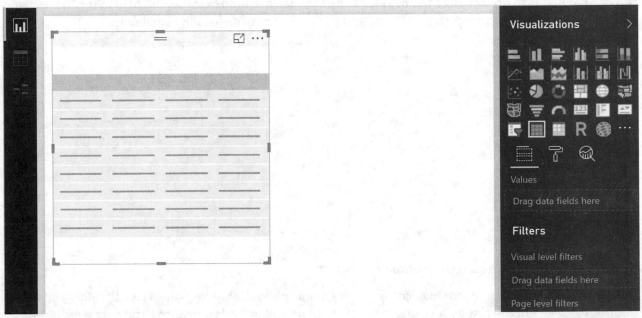

MarketKey	ProductKey	CalendarYearMonth	PoliticalGeographyKey	Units	Usage	SubscriberCount	RevenueAmount
467	22	201701	67	450	384.75	1	$12..
633	11	201706	33	450	384.75	1	$41..
335	27	201702	35	450	384.75	1	$30.
71	71	201702	71	450	384.75	1	$4..
461	1	201709	461	450	384.75	1	$50..
679	106	201709	79	450	384.75	1	$12..
695	57	201702	95	450	384.75	1	$30..
611	72	201706	11	450	384.75	1	$10..

Absolute Last Invoice Fiscal Date = LASTDATE(Invoice[Fiscal Date])

Figure 3.38: Adding a measure.

Jim wants this measure to always return the last date for which he has an invoice. To test that it works, he creates a matrix. He then selects the Report pane and selects the matrix visual.

Figure 3.39: Adding a visual.

Jim drags FyYear and FyMonth from the Calendar table in the Fields pane to the Values pane. He notices that he doesn't see the actual years and months but instead the total values. He also notices the sigma symbol in front of the fields in the Fields pane.

Figure 3.40: Additive values.

To change this behavior, he selects the column and changes the Default Summarization setting on the Modeling tab from Sum to Don't Summarize. The next time this field is used, it won't summarize the data.

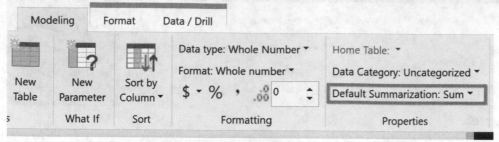

Figure 3.41: Changing the default summarization.

Now all Jim needs to do is change the field for this particular visual, so he clicks the field in the Values pane and selects Don't Summarize instead of Sum, and the change is made for this visual only.

FyYear	FyMonth
2014	7
2014	8
2014	9
2014	10
2014	11
2014	12
2015	1

Figure 3.42: Showing the data without summarizing it.

Now Jim adds the [Absolute Last Invoice Fiscal Date] measure to the Values pane as well. Unfortunately, this doesn't give Jim the results he expected: Instead of returning the last invoice fiscal date ever, it returns the last invoice fiscal date for *each* month in the table.

FyYear	FyMonth	Absolute Last Invoice Fiscal Date
2015	7	7/1/2015 12:00:00 AM
2015	8	8/1/2015 12:00:00 AM
2015	9	9/1/2015 12:00:00 AM
2015	10	10/1/2015 12:00:00 AM
2015	11	11/1/2015 12:00:00 AM
2015	12	12/1/2015 12:00:00 AM
2016	1	1/1/2016 12:00:00 AM
2016	2	2/1/2016 12:00:00 AM
2016	3	3/1/2016 12:00:00 AM
2016	4	4/1/2016 12:00:00 AM
2016	5	5/1/2016 12:00:00 AM
2016	6	6/1/2016 12:00:00 AM
2016	7	7/1/2016 12:00:00 AM
2016	8	8/1/2016 12:00:00 AM
2016	9	9/1/2016 12:00:00 AM
Total		**5/1/2018 12:00:00 AM**

Figure 3.43: Adding values to the matrix allows Jim to check the end result.

Data Model Tip: Filter Context and CALCULATE

DAX returns values filtered by whatever is selected on Rows, Columns, Filters, or Slicers. In DAX, this behavior is called *filter context*. In this case, the measure automatically filters the values of the measure for FyYear and FyMonth that are on Rows for the matrix.

FyYear	FyMonth	Absolute Last Invoice Fiscal Date
2015	7	7/1/2015 12:00:00 AM
2015	8	8/1/2015 12:00:00 AM
2015	9	9/1/2015 12:00:00 AM
2015	10	10/1/2015 12:00:00 AM
2015	11	11/1/2015 12:00:00 AM
2015	12	12/1/2015 12:00:00 AM
2016	1	1/1/2016 12:00:00 AM
2016	2	2/1/2016 12:00:00 AM
2016	3	3/1/2016 12:00:00 AM
2016	4	4/1/2016 12:00:00 AM
2016	5	5/1/2016 12:00:00 AM
2016	6	6/1/2016 12:00:00 AM
2016	7	7/1/2016 12:00:00 AM
2016	8	8/1/2016 12:00:00 AM
2016	9	9/1/2016 12:00:00 AM
Total		**5/1/2018 12:00:00 AM**

Figure 3.44: For the two highlighted rows, the LASTDATE formula returns only the last date for the month selected in the matrix.

Because filter context is the single most important concept in DAX, I want to spend a little time making sure you understand it. Imagine that you create a measure, like so:

```
[Sum of RevenueAmount]=
        SUM(Invoice[RevenueAmount])
```

This measure will add all the numbers in a column called Invoice[RevenueAmount]—but based on what? Look at what happens when you put this measure in a matrix.

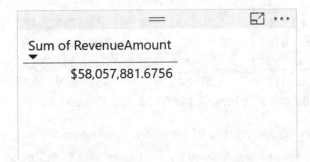

Figure 3.45: Just a measure inside a matrix.

When you put a measure in any visual without any fields on Rows or Columns, you get the sum for all the values of the Invoice[RevenueAmount] column for the entire table; that is, no filter is applied to the value.

Now look at what happens when you add Region to Rows.

Region	Sum of RevenueAmount
WEST	$32,081,622.0192
EAST	$17,897,819.8026
CENTRAL	$3,743,979.5893
NORTH	$3,670,210.705
SOUTH	$664,249.5595
Total	**$58,057,881.6756**

Figure 3.46: The same measure now shows a result for each region.

You expected this behavior, right? The values are now split out by region, with one grand total. How does this work? What happens here is that the same [Sum of RevenueAmount] measure is calculated six times: once with a filter on each region and once for the grand total. You can make it a little bit more interesting, as shown in Figure 3.47.

Region	2015	2016	2017	2018
WEST	$6,881,623.8166	$11,956,067.7048	$10,459,363.3793	$2,784,567.1185
EAST	$2,950,705.0084	$5,762,058.9869	$6,016,269.9526	$3,168,785.8547
CENTRAL	$286,994.4132	$976,531.6185	$1,551,512.1681	$928,941.3895
NORTH	$231,857.3424	$722,562.5354	$1,201,496.1727	$1,514,294.6545
SOUTH		$82,184.6177	$207,846.8411	$374,218.1007
Total	**$10,351,180.5806**	**$19,499,405.4633**	**$19,436,488.5138**	**$8,770,807.1179**

Figure 3.47: More values on Rows and Columns means the measure is executed more times.

Here the filter context for each cell in the matrix is more complex. For example, when you look at [Sum of RevenueAmount] for FyYear 2017 and Region North, you see a single cell in the table that is filtered by FyYear 2017 and Region North.

Region	2015	2016	2017	2018
WEST	$6,881,623.8166	$11,956,067.7048	$10,459,363.3793	$2,784,567.1185
EAST	$2,950,705.0084	$5,762,058.9869	$6,016,269.9526	$3,168,785.8547
CENTRAL	$286,994.4132	$976,531.6185	$1,551,512.1681	$928,941.3895
NORTH	$231,857.3424	$722,562.5354	$1,201,496.1727	$1,514,294.6545
SOUTH		$82,184.6177	$207,846.8411	$374,218.1007
Total	**$10,351,180.5806**	**$19,499,405.4633**	**$19,436,488.5138**	**$8,770,807.1179**

Figure 3.48: The value of [Sum of RevenueAmount] for FyYear 2017 is filtered by Region North.

What does this mean? Remember that all measures are filtered by whatever is put on Rows, Columns, Filters, and Slicers; this is the *filter context* of a measure. Imagine the filter context as a small submodel with data filtered by the values on Rows, Columns, Filters, and Slicers. This is the most important fundamental concept to grasp when writing DAX in Power BI, so you need to be sure you understand it.

Very importantly, you can put this behavior to use with DAX. Certain DAX functions allow you to tell the DAX engine to ignore a filter set by a report but to instead always use whatever you tell it to use.

The most powerful function in DAX is the CALCULATE function, which you use like this:

```
CALCULATE(<expression>,<filter1>,<filter2>...)
```

MSDN says that this function "evaluates an expression in a context that is modified by the speci-fied filters" (see **http://ppivot.us/ub50Z**). In other words, the CALCULATE function allows you to execute an expression and to express your own filters. Consider this example:

```
[Sum of RevenueAmount CALC]=
     CALCULATE(
          SUM([RevenueAmount])
          ,PoliticalGeography[Region]="North")
```

This tells the Power BI engine to set the filter of the SUM([RevenueAmount]) expression to PoliticalGeography[Region]="North", and in Figure 3.49 you can see what it looks like when you put this measure in a matrix.

Region	2015	2016	2017	2018
CENTRAL	$231,857.3424	$722,562.5354	$1,201,496.1727	$1,514,294.6545
EAST	$231,857.3424	$722,562.5354	$1,201,496.1727	$1,514,294.6545
NORTH	$231,857.3424	$722,562.5354	$1,201,496.1727	$1,514,294.6545
SOUTH	$231,857.3424	$722,562.5354	$1,201,496.1727	$1,514,294.6545
WEST	$231,857.3424	$722,562.5354	$1,201,496.1727	$1,514,294.6545
Total	**$231,857.3424**	**$722,562.5354**	**$1,201,496.1727**	**$1,514,294.6545**

Figure 3.49: Setting the filter argument of CALCULATE overrides any outside filters.

If you compare Figure 3.49 with Figure 3.48, you can see that the same row is repeated for each region—in this case the region North—but it is very important to observe that the FyYear column values are still filtered appropriately. So as soon as you add a field to the filter argument, any "out-side" filters on this field will be ignored, and the ones added to the measure will be used instead.

Here's another example:

```
[Sum of RevenueAmount CALC]=
     CALCULATE(
          SUM([RevenueAmount]),
          ALL(PoliticalGeography[Region]))
```

In this case, you tell the VertiPaq engine to set the filter of the SUM([RevenueAmount]) expression to *all* values of PoliticalGeography[Region], effectively removing the filter each time the measure is executed.

Region	15	2016	2017	2018
CENTRAL	$10,351,180.5806	$19,499,405.4633	$19,436,488.5138	$8,770,807.1179
EAST	$10,351,180.5806	$19,499,405.4633	$19,436,488.5138	$8,770,807.1179
NORTH	$10,351,180.5806	$19,499,405.4633	$19,436,488.5138	$8,770,807.1179
SOUTH	$10,351,180.5806	$19,499,405.4633	$19,436,488.5138	$8,770,807.1179
WEST	$10,351,180.5806	$19,499,405.4633	$19,436,488.5138	$8,770,807.1179
Total	**$0,351,180.5806**	**$19,499,405.4633**	**$19,436,488.5138**	**$8,770,807.1179**

Figure 3.50: Using ALL as a filter in CALCULATE has the effect of removing the filter for each cell.

Filter context and the CALCULATE function are your main tools for getting the most out of Power BI and DAX. *DAX Formulas for Power Pivot* by Rob Collie goes into more details on filter context (**http://ppivot.us/gYukh**), and so does *The Definitive Guide to DAX* by Marco Russo and Alberto Ferrari (**http://ppivot.us/daxge2**).

Jim changes his measure to make sure the last date for the entire table is calculated:

```
[Absolute Last Invoice Fiscal Date]=
    CALCULATE(
        LASTDATE(Invoice[Fiscal Date])
        , ALL(Invoice)
        )
```

> CALCULATE and ALL tell the engine to always calculate the last date of the Invoice[Date] column for all the rows in the Invoice table, thus ignoring any filters.

Data Model Tip: Formatting Measures

The formula bar in Power BI Desktop allows you to format your DAX calculations in order to improve the readability of your measures. The following are a few examples of common practices:

- Start a new line (by pressing Alt+Enter) for each new function or function parameter.

- Indent a newly started line to either start where the previous function ended or, in the case of function parameters, start at the same position as the previous parameter. You can use either the Tab key or spaces to achieve this indentation.

- In the case of multiple parameters, start a new line with a comma.

- If you want more horizontal space, you might want to start a new line right after the measure name. This book follows this practice for the sake of brevity, but when writing DAX measures outside the book, I don't start a new line after the measure name.

These common practices are not mandatory, but they can help you write more readable measures.

Jim goes back to his matrix and observes that now the same value is returned for all the rows.

FyYear	FyMonth	Absolute Last Invoice Fiscal Date
2014	12	5/1/2018 12:00:00 AM
2015	1	5/1/2018 12:00:00 AM
2015	2	5/1/2018 12:00:00 AM
2015	3	5/1/2018 12:00:00 AM

Figure 3.51: The last date is now calculated for the entire Invoice table.

Now Jim needs to add to the Calendar table a new column that he can use in his filters to select the current fiscal year. He creates two new calculated columns in the Calendar table to check the current fiscal year. This is the first one:

```
[CurrentFyYear]=
    IF(
        [FyYear]=YEAR([Absolute Last Invoice Fiscal Date])
        ,1
        ,0
        )
```

> Keep in mind that Jim is creating calculated columns, not measures, so it is possible to use them as filters in the Filters pane.

His first calculated column returns 1 if the value from the FyYear column is the same as the year part returned by the [Absolute Last Invoice Fiscal Date] measure.

Jim creates another function to add a calculated column that returns 1 when the row in the Calendar table is the current fiscal month:

```
[CurrentFyMonth]=
    IF(
        [FyYear]=YEAR([Absolute Last Invoice Fiscal Date])
        &&
        [FyMonth]=MONTH([Absolute Last Invoice Fiscal Date])
        ,1
        ,0
    )
```

These calculated columns compare the values from the current FyYear and FyMonth columns in the DateTable table with the year and month returned by the [Last Invoice Fiscal Date] measure. If the values are the same, the measure returns 1; otherwise, it returns 0. Jim switches to the data view to see all the data in the table and verify the changes.

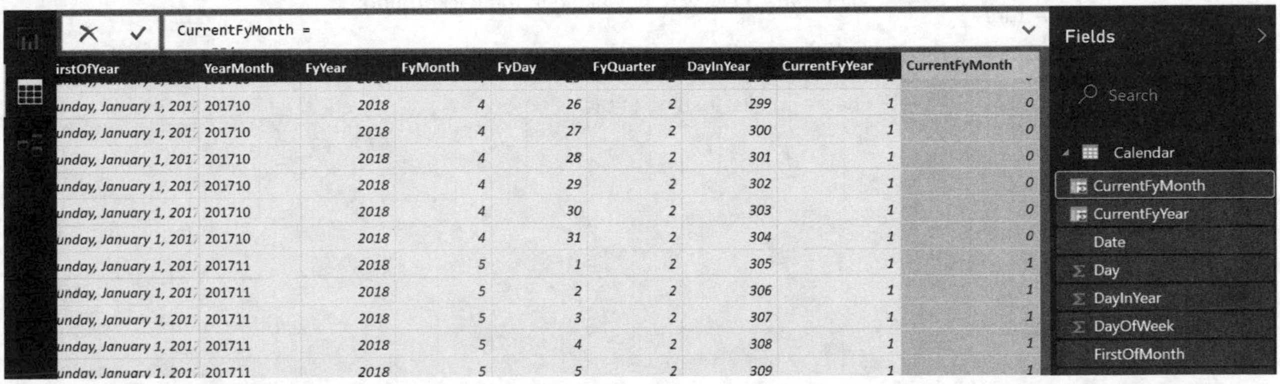

Figure 3.52: The formulas in the calculated columns will be evaluated every time the data is refreshed.

Now that Jim has created the relationships and enriched the data model with additional columns, he can focus on other aspects of the model that he needs to add to get the results requested by the business. Jim has anticipated that he needs to add many measures that are date related—for example, calculations using running total, previous month, and year-to-date.

Data Model Tip: The Time Intelligence Functions

DAX contains many functions that make working with time easier. These functions are called the *time intelligence functions*.

Working with the time intelligence functions can be quite difficult for a novice DAX user. To make working with these functions easier, you can apply the following "golden rules" to any model (see **http://ppivot.us/DYBUJ**):

1. *Turn off the Auto Date/Time feature.*

If you don't have a calendar table, Power BI will automatically create one for you. On import, it will automatically detect all the date columns in the model and create a new date table for every date column in your model. You can then use years, months, and days automatically in the Power BI interface. This is great for some simple or quick analytics but doesn't allow you to extend and customize your calendar in any way. It also takes up a lot of memory, as described at **http://ppivot.us/ydfes2d**.

In general, I recommend using these built-in date tables only when doing quick analytics, and I recommend using your own calendar table when doing more serious analytics. It is simple to turn off the auto-generated date tables. Select File, Options, Data Load, and under Time Intelligence, deselect Auto Date/Time.

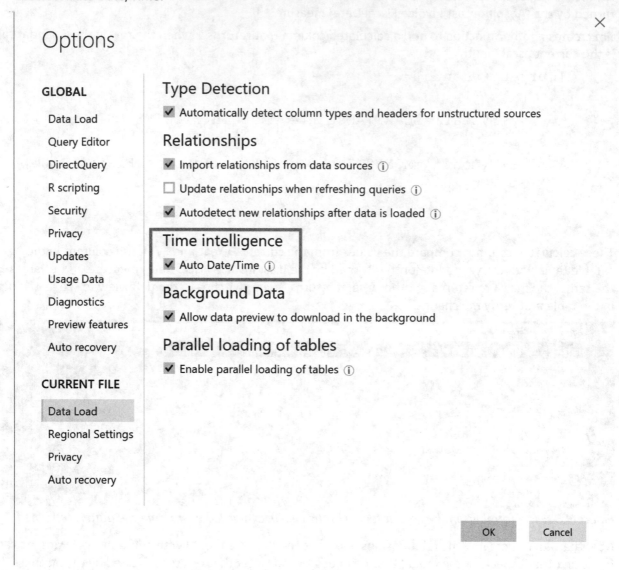

Figure 3.53: Turning off the Auto Date/Time feature.

2. Never use a date column from a fact table as a date argument in time intelligence functions.

Remember the filter context concept discussed a little bit earlier in this chapter? Imagine that you add Years to Rows for your matrix. Power BI would automatically filter the row context down to contain only values of the year for the current row in your matrix. If you then want to compare with a previous year, you need to overwrite that filter context because it can only access the selected year. This is possible with DAX but can quickly become very cumbersome. When you follow this rule—and avoid using a date column from a fact table as a date column in DAX time functions—you don't have to worry about this issue because the functions will take care of over-riding the filters automatically.

3. Always create a separate date table.

The date table should consist of at least a date column that covers the first and last dates you want to report on and any columns that you want to use in your report, such as year and month. This is usually the date argument that you can use with your time intelligence functions.

4. Make sure your date table includes a continuous date range.

DAX uses the date column to navigate through time. Say that you have selected January 2018 in a table, and you want to show the sales for the preceding year. DAX will automatically determine the date range for January 2018, using your date table, and then it will use that date range to determine the date range for January 2017. If the date table is missing some dates in January 2017, the results will be missing data for the same day the previous year, which might mean that some sales are now missing.

5. Create relationships between fact tables and the date table.

After you create relationships, you can use values from the date table in your visuals. This is great if you want to filter your data by year or month or even fiscal year instead of the date directly.

6. The date column in the date table should be at day granularity (without fractions of a day).

DAX doesn't support dates smaller than day granularity. It is often a good idea to remove the time parts of dates for performance and compression reasons.

Jim selects both the Date and Fiscal Date columns from the Invoice table and hides them. He does this to ensure that he doesn't use the date fields from the Invoice table directly but rather uses the columns from the Calendar table. Even though both columns will be hidden in the Fields pane, they can still be used in DAX formulas.

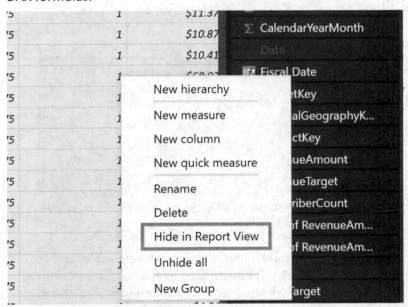

Figure 3.54: Always hide columns that you think you will not use in a report.

Jim plans to use the Calendar table that is available in his data source because it meets all the requirements. He has also created a relationship between the Calendar table and his fact table.

Jim has now prepared his model to use time intelligence functions.

Jim needs to report over the past 12 months. Instead of solving this problem by using a calculation, Jim decides to add to the Calendar table another calculated column that he can use as a filter on his visuals. He needs to use the regular date to make sure the right months will be selected, so he adds the following measure:

```
[Absolute Last Invoice Date] =
    CALCULATE (
        LASTDATE (Invoice[Date])
        , ALL (Invoice)
        )
```

This measure allows Jim to create a new column that dynamically calculates the past 12 months as a calculated column:

```
[Running 12 FY months]=
    IF(
        [Date] >= EOMONTH(
                [Absolute Last Invoice Date]
                ,-12
            )+1
        &&
        [Date] <= EOMONTH(
                [Absolute Last Invoice Date]
                ,0
            )
        ,1
        ,0)
```

> This calculated column returns 1 when the date value is between the first day of the month 12 months before the last invoice date and the end of the month of the last invoice date.

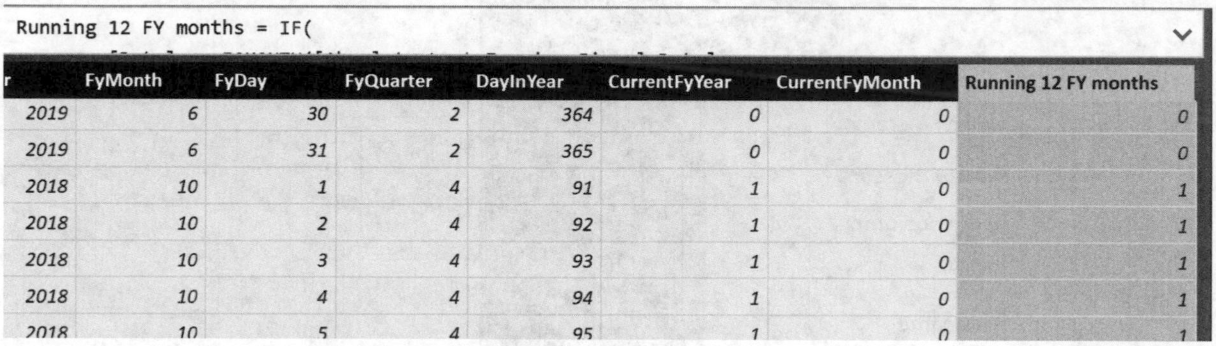

```
Running 12 FY months = IF(                                                              ⌄
```

r	FyMonth	FyDay	FyQuarter	DayInYear	CurrentFyYear	CurrentFyMonth	Running 12 FY months
2019	6	30	2	364	0	0	0
2019	6	31	2	365	0	0	0
2018	10	1	4	91	1	0	1
2018	10	2	4	92	1	0	1
2018	10	3	4	93	1	0	1
2018	10	4	4	94	1	0	1
2018	10	5	4	95	1	0	1

Figure 3.55: The formulas in the calculated column will be evaluated every time the data is refreshed.

Jim will now be able to use these calculated columns in his reports to make his life a little easier.

During the two days that Jim was working on preparing the model, new data became available, and Jim needs that new data in his dashboard. Power BI Desktop makes it easy to load new data. Jim can simply select Refresh on the Home tab. Refreshing the data also causes the calculated columns to recalculate. So, for example, when new invoices with later dates are loaded into the model, [CurrentFyMonth] might return different values.

Jim has now prepared his model, and he is ready to start doing analytics and create his dashboard.

4 - Building the Main Report

In this chapter Jim creates the main report in Power BI Desktop, using the data model he set up in Chapter 3. He then creates various data visualizations needed for his report and uses DAX formulas to get the values he needs. This report will provide a basis for the detailed reports Jim will create in the next chapter.

Getting Set Up

Now that Jim has prepared the layout of his model, he is ready to start designing and creating a main report. Later he will create more reports that provide detailed information around particular subject areas. He will also build a dashboard to summarize the most important information.

Jim knows he needs to collect some basic information to display on the report, and in order to determine what to collect, he must answer questions like these:

- What is the last date for which we have data that is used in the report? How fresh is the data?
- What are the current year and month we are reporting on?

The Power BI Desktop file right now has some pages with data used to validate the measures he created earlier. Jim adds a new page and renames it Overview. He then deletes the other pages because he doesn't need them anymore.

Jim wants to show the last invoice date, which will help him display the last date for which there is data in the report. He already added the [Absolute Last Invoice Date] measure (see Chapter 3), which will help him with this.

To display the measure in his reports, Jim wants to make sure the reports show the values in the correct format, so he sets the format of the measure to M/D/YY by selecting Format on the Modeling tab and then selecting the format shown in Figure 4.1.

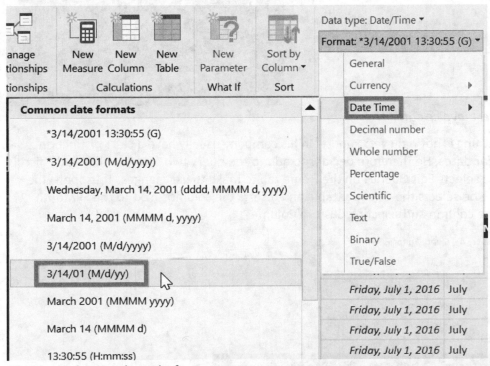

Figure 4.1: Setting the right format.

When you set the formatting in a measure, the field stores that formatting. Thereafter, every time you use that measure, the same formatting will be applied. You can, however, overrule this automatically applied formatting on the visual.

Now Jim goes back to the overview page to verify that it works as expected. He clicks the matrix visual in the Visualizations pane. In the Rows area, he adds FyYear and FyMonth, and in the Values area, he adds Absolute Last Invoice Date. He then adds CurrentFyMonth under Visual Level Filters and selects the value 1 to filter this visual to show just the current fiscal year's month. Year and Month are nested values in the matrix, but Jim wants to see all the values, so he selects the button that expands everything down one level in the hierarchy on the visual. Now Jim can see the values he can use in his report.

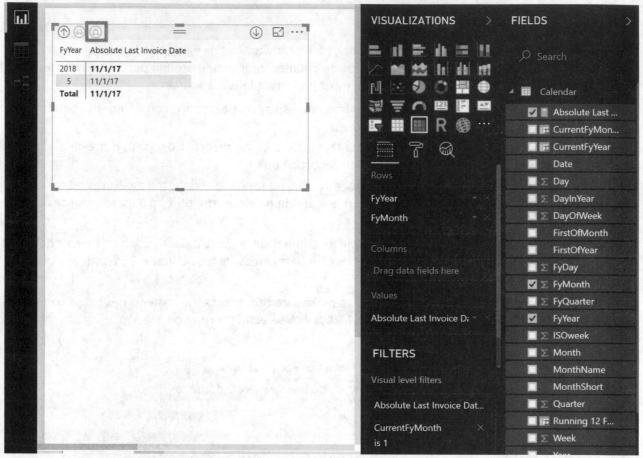

Figure 4.2: Getting the latest invoice date.

But Jim notices that something is not right yet: Reports in his company usually have a clear distinction between fiscal and calendar dates. He therefore decides to add to the query two columns that add a fiscal year label to his model. He selects Edit Queries on the Home tab to make these changes. This opens the Power Query Editor, where he selects the Calendar table and inserts the columns next to the FyMonth column by right-clicking the column and selecting Custom Column.

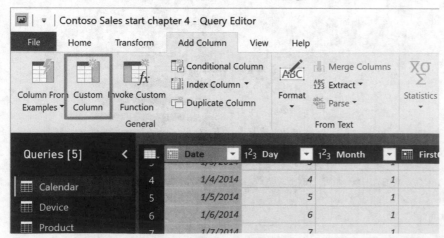

Figure 4.3: Inserting a custom column between two columns in the Power Query Editor.

> To make any changes in the Power Query Editor, you need to have access to the data source, so I have already added these columns to the sample file.

Jim uses three custom column formulas to get the correct labels. This is the first one:

```
[FyYearLabel]=
  "FY" & Text.End(Number.ToText([FyYear]),2)
```

> This formula adds the text FY before the last two characters of the FyYear column.

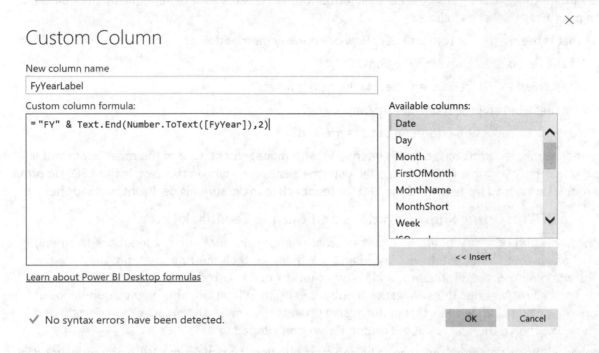

Learn about Power BI Desktop formulas

✓ No syntax errors have been detected.   OK   Cancel

Figure 4.4: Entering the custom column formula.

This is the second formula:

```
[FyMonthLabel]=
  "M" & Text.PadStart(Text.From([FyMonth]),2,"0")
```

> This formula adds the text M before the FyMonth column and adds a trailing 0 when the month is only one character.

This is the third formula:

```
[FyQuarterLabel]=
  "Q"&Text.From([FyQuarter])
```

> This formula adds the text Q before the value in the FyQuarter column.

When he is done adding the new columns, Jim clicks Close & Apply on the Home tab of the Power Query Editor, and the new columns are added to the model. Jim can now swap out the FyYear and FyMonth columns for the new FyYearLabel and FyMonthLabel columns, and he sees the updated terminology used in the matrix.

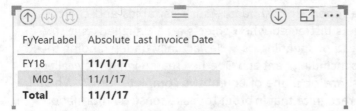

Figure 4.5: Fiscal year labels added to the matrix.

Creating the Report

Jim has prepared his model to the point where he can now start creating the actual report, but before he does so, he needs to plan it.

The goal of Jim's dashboard is to help the management team get quick insights from all data—from HR to sales to the pipeline. Jim needs to do a deep dive into the sales data, which will later be recapped into a dashboard where users can choose a few important metrics (see Chapter 6).

To make sure he shows the right sales-related information, Jim creates a list of all requests the board made and then prioritizes the list as follows:

1. What is the rhythm of the business? How are our key metrics doing?

2. Did the revenue pick up for all regions?

3. Did the new PR effort have an effect in the new markets?

4. What are our top products? Are they improving?

5. Did the cost reduction effort pan out as expected?

Jim has made some decisions based on his interviews with management. One of the most important lessons he has learned over time is to iterate often with the customer—who in this case is the CFO. He often sends out quick emails to his team and the CFO for feedback to make sure his decisions work for her.

Power BI Tip: Doing Short Iterations and Getting Feedback Often

As the creation of a dashboard or report is progressing, make sure you get feedback from end users. Show them what you have created and ask them for their input. In the end, they are the ones who will use the dashboard, and it's your job to make sure the information is conveyed appropriately. It's better to get negative feedback early than later on, after you've done a lot of work. Also, by including the users in the design process, you make them part of the design, and they will embrace the end result even more if they contributed to it.

Jim removes all the visuals from the page so he can start building the real report. With any report or dashboard, it is very important to make sure you keep it clean and organized. To help with this, Jim turns on Show Gridlines and Snap Objects to Grid in the View tab of Power BI Desktop.

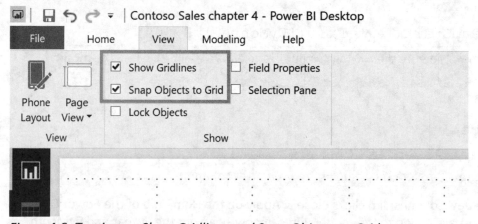

Figure 4.6: Turning on Show Gridlines and Snap Objects to Grid.

Visualization Tip: Designing a Clean Report

Good alignment of the major objects on a report or dashboard—such as tables and charts—makes a big difference. The human brain gets distracted when objects aren't aligned as it subconsciously tries to align those objects instead of spending its cycles actually understanding the objects. In the 1920s, German psychologists including Kant and Goethe created what they called *gestalt theories*. *Gestalt* is German for "essence or shape of an entity's complete form." When applied to visual perception, these theories recognize that in order to make sense of information, the human brain tries to organize the information in a particular way. When we humans look at a combination of visuals, we see the whole before we see the individual parts that make up that whole.

Early 20th-century psychologists determined that the fundamental principle of gestalt perception is the law of grouping. This law says that we tend to order our experience in a manner that is regular, orderly, symmetric, and simple. Those psychologists determined a number of principles that, in theory, would allow us to predict how a total visual is interpreted, including proximity, similarity, closure, symmetry, common fate, continuity, good gestalt, and experience. Following these principles helps create a harmonious design that looks and feels right to the user. In recent years, these principles have become more and more important in the design world; many great designers use them intuitively.

What does gestalt have to do with you? And how does it relate to the work you do in Power BI? Well, a complete study of this subject would fill a book on its own, but here we can look at two important ideas that everyone should be able to apply:

- **Keep related data close:** If you have a matrix with revenue by region on your dashboard and you also have a chart that contains regions and revenue that either tells a different story or that supports the information on the matrix, make sure this information is grouped together. Such grouping reduces friction for the user: Seeing the same or similar information in close proximity makes it easier to understand. You may need to restructure a report or dashboard after you add additional pieces, and that can be a chore. But I assure you it's well worth the effort.

- **Check your alignment:** Make sure all tables and charts are aligned and, if possible, of equal width and height. This will give your dashboard a much cleaner look and make it easier for the user to "grok" the information. Here a few simple tips for getting good alignment: First of all, when possible, align all your charts and tables to the same gridlines when placed above or next to each other. If you set Snap Objects to Grid, it will be easier to align them on the page with other charts and tables. When everything is set to align to the page grid, it's a piece of cake to make objects the same width. Sometimes you need to get creative with charts to make them fit, but again, doing so is well worth it. Also, don't be afraid to leave some empty space between charts or tables; it's better to have some empty space than to cram together your visuals.

If you follow these two simple guidelines, your reports will be much easier to understand and read.

The following two figures show how you can quickly and easily get great results from some simple alignment.

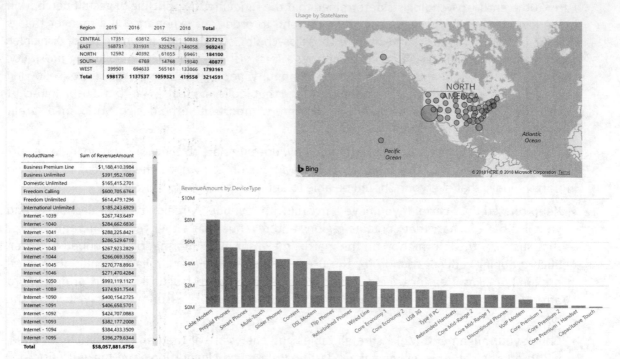

Figure 4.7: A busy report that's not aligned.

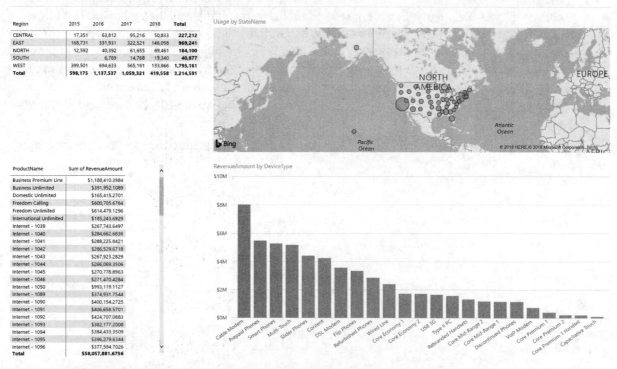

Figure 4.8: The same report, now neat and organized.

One of the main proponents of clean, well-designed reports and dashboards is Stephen Few. His books *Information Dashboard Design* (**http://ppivot.us/fds543s**) and *Show Me the Numbers* (**http://ppivot.us/fw43s4s**) cover this in great detail and are must-reads for every business analyst.

Next, Jim adds a title to the dashboard—Strategic Targets Overview—and two important labels to show when the data was refreshed last (Data As Of:) and identify the current reporting period (Reporting Period:). For this he uses three separate text boxes, and he chooses a light color for the text.

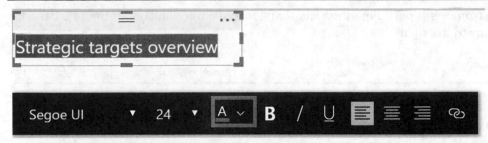

Figure 4.9: Adding the main title by using a text box.

The color for the title in Figure 4.9 is #8497b0. It can be set by using custom colors under the text color option, which is highlighted in Figure 4.9.

Visualization Tip: Choosing the Right Colors for a Dashboard

It is important to spend time thinking about the colors you want to use in a report or dashboard. Colors can be grouped into two types: aggressive and passive. Aggressive colors (such as red and green) attract attention immediately and imply importance, while passive colors (such as light gray) are soothing to the eye.

You don't want to attract attention to anything in your dashboard that doesn't warrant it. For example, using big bright labels with all uppercase and bold font will attract the eyes away from the actual data presented.

THIS TEXT   This text

Figure 4.10: The brighter, all-uppercase label attracts the eye immediately.

Contextual data such as labels should never compete with the actual data on a report. Such labels provide additional information that a user needs only when learning what data the report displays.

If you use color to attract the user's attention, make sure to use it sparingly. Otherwise, the user will get used to it, and it will no longer be a differentiator.

It's a good idea to define a set of colors that you want to use for a dashboard up front and try to add new colors to the set only when needed. A good way to get consistent colors is to create a Power BI theme and apply it to all your reports (see **http://ppivot.us/th34sd3**).

Jim wants to create a workbook that looks crisp and is easily readable, so he plans to use just one font for his dashboard: Segoe UI. In this case, the text Jim adds is a header, and he increases the font size to 24; for the other text boxes, he chooses a smaller size, 14.

Visualization Tip: Using Fonts

The same principles you need to consider with colors apply to fonts as well. For example, using too many fonts will distract a user from the information that you want to display. Before you start working on a dashboard or report, decide what fonts to use and stick to a maximum of two of them to reduce distraction.

While working on this book, I stumbled across research from MIT which found that a badly chosen font for a car dashboard can distract you from the road and increase your chance of crashing (see **http://ppivot.us/SSFPC**). This is a good lesson in how important typography can be.

Another factor that might be important is that a dashboard may need to use a business's standard typography and colors. Does the company have a default font? Maybe even colors? The CFO and CIO usually spend a lot of planning time and money on the website or corporate style and typically like it if they see these settings used in company reports as well. It's usually easy to find a company's colors, typography, and styling by looking at its website.

To clearly separate the title from the report, Jim uses a line shape to add a thick line under the title bar and adds the logo of the company to the right.

Strategic targets overview   Data as of: Reporting period:

Figure 4.11: Creating the header.

> A change from the default that I have made for this book is to set the page size to 4:3 instead of the default 16:9. This allowed me to make better screenshots to fit the book format. Changing this setting can be done in the Page Size properties on the Format pane. You can change from the Fields pane to the Format pane by selecting the little paint roller that is shown in Figure 4.12. For more on the Format pane, see **http://ppivot.us/pspbi23**.

Jim uses the [Absolute Last Invoice Date] measure from the Calendar table to display the last date the data was refreshed. He adds it to the report as a card. To format it, he opens the Format tab and sets the font to Segoe UI with size 14 and then deselects Category Label.

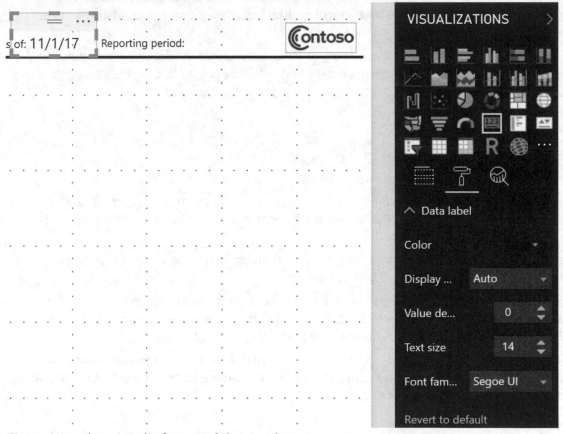

Figure 4.12: Changing the format of the visual.

When this is finalized, Jim positions the card visual next to the text box. He temporarily turns off Snap Objects to Grid and uses the Ctrl key and arrow keys on his keyboard to do the fine maneuvering of the visual.

> You will see how to add the Reporting Period: label later in this chapter.

Jim is now ready to add the first piece of data to the report. In one of the interview sessions, he learned that revenue isn't equal for all regions. It is very important for the management team to keep an eye on the revenue by region. Therefore, Jim wants to add revenue, the revenue variance-to-target, the year-over-year change for the current month, and the variance-to-target trend over time by region for the current month.

The company uses several acronyms in its reports, including $VTT for variance-to-target in dollars and YoY% for year-over-year change in percentage. Jim will use these in the dashboards and reports.

Jim drags a matrix onto the overview page to visualize the data by region.

Figure 4.13: Inserting a matrix.

Visualization Tip: Keeping Space Around the Edges

Using space well when visualizing data is an important art. Without the appropriate amount of space, a report looks too dense and busy. Make sure you keep the appropriate space between visuals and the edge of the report.

Jim now adds the Region field from the PoliticalGeography table to Rows on the matrix, and he adds RevenueAmount and RevenueTarget from the Invoice table under Values. The columns that are dragged into the Values area are automatically aggregated for each region; in this case, they are aggregated using SUM.

One of the primary values that Jim wants to display in the dashboard and reports is the sum of revenue. Instead of using the built-in SUM function, he creates a measure that he will be able to use as a base for other measures. He creates the new measure by right-clicking the Invoice table in the Fields pane and selecting New Measure. The formula bar opens, and Jim can write his new measure.

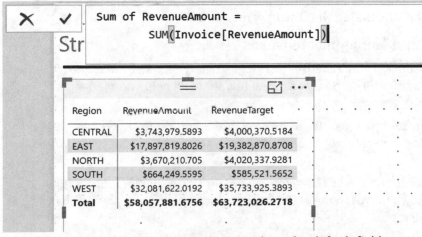

Figure 4.14: Creating a new measure to replace the default fields.

Jim creates the following measure:

```
[Sum of Revenue] =
    SUM([RevenueAmount])
```

He also creates a measure for revenue target:

```
[Sum of RevenueTarget] =
    SUM([RevenueTarget])
```

For both of these measures, Jim uses the Modeling tab to set the format to currency and the number of decimal places to two.

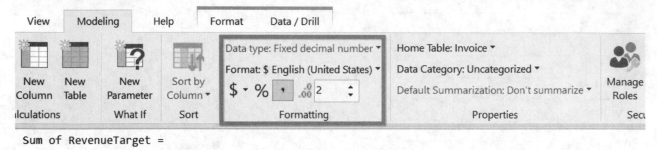

```
Sum of RevenueTarget =
  SUM([Revenuetarget])
```

Region	Sum of Revenue	Sum of RevenueTarget
CENTRAL	$176,989.31	$154,005.25
EAST	$621,381.14	$507,861.38
NORTH	$437,551.91	$391,540.54
SOUTH	$178,088.65	$136,230.05
WEST	$426,652.55	$349,042.05

Figure 4.15: Formatting the measure.

Now he replaces the columns from the Values area with the new measures.

Data Model Tip: Creating and Managing Measures

As a model gets more complex and you add more business logic to it, it becomes more and more important that you manage your measures. Here are a few tips that will help you manage large models that contain complex measures:

- Split a complex measure into several separate measures. When you do this, you can create and debug parts of the calculation separately. You might also be able to reuse measures, which makes mistakes less likely.

- Choose similar names for calculations over the same base field (for example, [Sum of Revenue], [Count of Revenue], [Revenue YoY%], and [Revenue to Target]). You can always change the name that appears on the report.

- Name a measure as clearly as possible to describe what it does.

- Hide measures that are not directly used or useful in reports (for example, intermediate measures). Hidden measures can still be referenced by DAX calculations.

- Format measures appropriately to save work later and ensure that the numbers are perceived correctly.

Because the reports need to show the current month, Jim uses the calculated column he created earlier to set the report filter to CurrentFyMonth. He turns off the Grand Total row by selecting the matrix and then setting Row Totals to Off under Subtotals in the Format pane. The table now looks as shown in Figure 4.16.

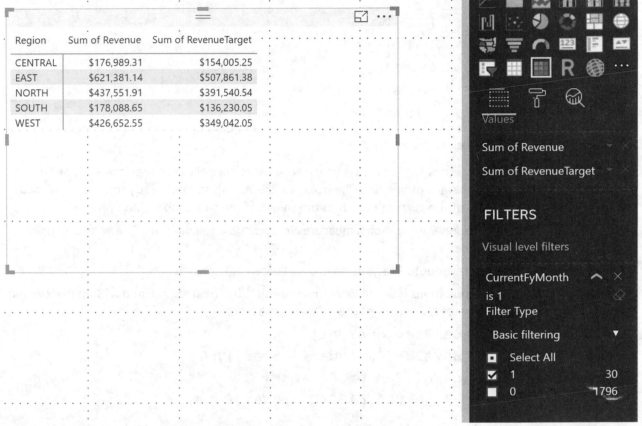

Figure 4.16: Adding fields to the matrix.

Instead of showing the revenue and its target directly, Jim wants to show the variance-to-target, so he adds a new measure with the following expression:

```
[Revenue to target]=
    [Sum of Revenue] - [Sum of RevenueTarget]
```

This expression calculates the variance-to-target for each region when put in the matrix, with Region under Rows.

Region	Sum of Revenue	Sum of RevenueTarget	Revenue to target
CENTRAL	$176,989.31	$154,005.25	$22,984.06
EAST	$621,381.14	$507,861.38	$113,519.76
NORTH	$437,551.91	$391,540.54	$46,011.37
SOUTH	$178,088.65	$136,230.05	$41,858.61
WEST	$426,652.55	$349,042.05	$77,610.50

Figure 4.17: Also adding the [Revenue to target] measure to the matrix.

Now Jim removes the Sum of RevenueTarget column from the matrix.

Next, Jim wants to add some styling. He decides to apply 9-point Segoe UI font to the matrix, so he selects the matrix and on the Format pane he changes the font size for both the column and row headers and the Values area. Next, he wants to change the style of the matrix to a clean and tidy look, so he selects Minimal under the Style property on the Format Pane.

Region	Sum of Revenue	Revenue to target
CENTRAL	$176,989.31	$22,984.06
EAST	$621,381.14	$113,519.76
NORTH	$437,551.91	$46,011.37
SOUTH	$178,088.65	$41,858.61
WEST	$426,652.55	$77,610.50

Figure 4.18: Formatting applied to the matrix.

One of the most important metrics for Contoso is year-over-year change. Jim's model is already set up correctly to follow the golden rules of time intelligence (see Chapter 3), so he is ready to create a measure that will compare the values of the current month to the values of the same month last year.

Jim knows it's a good idea to separate complex measures into multiple calculations. The year-over-year growth formula is quite simple:

(Current revenue - Previous revenue) / Previous revenue = Percentage growth

Jim already has current revenue in his [Sum of Revenue] measure, but he needs to add a [Sum of Revenue PreviousYear] measure. Therefore, Jim creates the following measure:

```
[Sum of Revenue PreviousYear] =
    IF(SELECTEDVALUE(Calendar[FyYear]),
        CALCULATE([Sum of Revenue]
                ,DATEADD(Calendar[Date]
                ,-1
                ,YEAR
                )
            )
        )
```

> This measure determines the sum of revenue for the dates in the current cell of the visual and uses the DATEADD function to move those dates back one year in time, based on the values in the Calendar table. Jim wants to make sure that when this calculation is used in other reports, it won't throw an error when DAX is unable to find the right dates. He therefore uses the SELECTEDVALUE function to check whether the current cell contains only one value returned for the Calendar[FyYear] column. The else argument of the IF function is optional; when it is omitted, DAX automatically returns BLANK.

Data Model Tip: BLANK Values?

A blank value, an empty cell, and a missing value are all represented by a special value type: BLANK. Why is this important? One of the main characteristics of working with data in Power BI is that, by default, blank values are never shown in visuals. By using the DAX BLANK() function to return a BLANK value, you can determine whether you want Power BI to show something for the row or column for which the calculation is evaluated. This behavior is similar to behavior in Excel. (A blank value is treated a little differently in DAX than in Excel, however. For more details, see **http://ppivot.us/JYCSL**.)

Next, Jim makes sure the format is set to currency with two decimal places.

Data Model Tip: Understanding How Time Intelligence Functions Work

What does it mean when I say that the calculation above will calculate the sum of revenue shifted backward in time by one year from the dates in the current context?

When you use time intelligence functions such as `DATEADD` and `SAMEPERIODLASTYEAR`, DAX tries to determine the dates for the currently selected period in the current cell. The following example shows the sum of revenue by fiscal year (in the boxes) and by fiscal month (underlined).

FyYearLabel	Sum of Revenue
FY17	$19,436,488.51
M01	$1,609,312.88
M02	$1,648,915.76
M03	$1,781,446.87
M04	$1,705,202.55
M05	$1,623,453.75
M06	$1,756,153.29
M07	$1,550,087.81
M08	$1,468,985.39
M09	$1,463,013.24
M10	$1,568,567.87
M11	$1,596,141.88
M12	$1,665,207.22
FY18	$8,770,807.12
M01	$1,706,178.98
M02	$1,669,749.41
M03	$1,736,790.86
M04	$1,817,424.32
M05	$1,840,663.56
Total	**$28,207,295.63**

Figure 4.19: Showing the context.

DAX tries to use the dates in the Calendar table that are set up using the time intelligence golden rules to determine what period is selected in the range for the current cell. It recognizes the boxed values to be by year and the underlined ones to be by month. DAX is able to recognize years, quarters, months, and days. It uses the start and end dates for the entire period in the Calendar table to traverse backward or forward in time; it does not use the actual dates that you have as values. In this example, notice that FY18 has only five months' worth of data, but this does not mean that DAX will use only those five months when getting the data for the previous year; it will use the entire year because for the year selection, the entire period is selected. For FY18 in this table, the last seven months don't have data yet, so they are not shown on a month level.

Figure 4.20 shows what happens when you add the previous year formula to the matrix.

FyYearLabel	Sum of Revenue	Sum of Revenue PreviousYear
FY17	**$19,436,488.51**	**$19,499,405.46**
M01	$1,609,312.88	$1,706,391.03
M02	$1,648,915.76	$1,696,727.20
M03	$1,781,446.87	$1,690,528.11
M04	$1,705,202.55	$1,676,105.52
M05	$1,623,453.75	$1,664,064.20
M06	$1,756,153.29	$1,772,804.54
M07	$1,550,087.81	$1,638,170.46
M08	$1,468,985.39	$1,626,721.29
M09	$1,463,013.24	$1,382,612.06
M10	$1,568,567.87	$1,419,125.71
M11	$1,596,141.88	$1,615,586.60
M12	$1,665,207.22	$1,610,568.74
FY18	**$8,770,807.12**	**$19,436,488.51**
M01	$1,706,178.98	$1,609,312.88
M02	$1,669,749.41	$1,648,915.76
M03	$1,736,790.86	$1,781,446.87
M04	$1,817,424.32	$1,705,202.55
M05	$1,840,663.56	$1,623,453.75
M06		$1,756,153.29
M07		$1,550,087.81

Figure 4.20: Shifting dates.

Now you can clearly see that for each cell, DAX uses the date range of the current cell to traverse time. This is one of the important reasons for including in your model a separate date table that contains a continuous date range.

For more information on this and similar concepts, see **http://ppivot.us/KQSEF**.

Jim wants to hide the measure he just created because he doesn't want this field to clutter the Fields pane. He does so by right-clicking the field and selecting Hide.

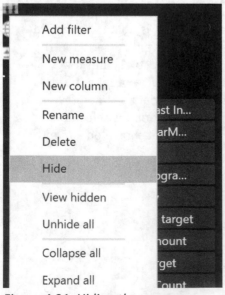

Figure 4.21: Hiding the measure.

Data Model Tip: Variables

Variables are a new construct in DAX, introduced at the same time as Power BI. Variables allow you to split up a measure into several calculations within the formula itself. Using variables has two major benefits:

- It makes a complicated measure much more readable.

- It improves performance. The results of the expressions are stored as named variables. This means that if you want to use the same expression multiple times in your formula, it gets executed only once instead of multiple times, as would be the case if you referenced the expression directly.

You use the VAR statement to assign an expression to a named variable. For a simple scenario, it might look like this:

```
[Calculation]=
    //Define the Sales variable
    VAR Sales = [Sum of SalesAmount]
    //Define the SalesAllTime variable
    VAR SalesAllTime = CALCULATE([Sum of SalesAmount]
                                ,ALL(Calendar)
    //Return the outcome of the measure
    RETURN IF(NOT(ISBLANK(Sales))
                                ,DIVIDE(
                                Sales
                                ,SalesAllTime
                                )

        )
```

You might wonder why the Sales variable isn't used in the SalesAllTime variable definition. This is because a filter context change cannot be applied to the outcome of a variable. In the SalesAllTime variable the outcome of the sum of salesamount value isn't used, we ask the engine to calculate sum of salesamount for a different filter content.

As you can see, this example uses the Sales variable twice, but the data model will have to calculate the results only once. This is a very simple expression, so the performance difference might be negligible, but in complicated expressions, using VAR can be very efficient.

Data Model Tip: Comments

In Power BI, it is possible to add comments to your formulas. If you start a line with //, the language parser will ignore the rest of the line, and you can type anything you want to annotate your expressions. You can also use /* to start a comment and then */ to end it. This is the method to use when you want a comment to span multiple lines.

Comments can be very useful in complicated scenarios or when you work on a project with multiple people as they can help keep track of the meaning or purpose for each calculation.

Next, Jim creates the year-over-year calculation:

```
[Sum of Revenue YoY%] =
VAR Revenue = [Sum of Revenue]
VAR Revenueprevyear = [Sum of Revenue PreviousYear]
RETURN IF(
        NOT(ISBLANK(Revenue)),
            DIVIDE(
                (Revenue
                    - Revenueprevyear)
                ,Revenueprevyear
            )
        )
```

This calculation determines the year-over-year change when [Sum of Revenue] is not empty for the current cell; if it is empty, the formula returns BLANK. You would want to add such a test for empty values with time periods in the future when you have values for the previous year but not for the current time period; when this is the case, Power BI returning BLANK will show a skewed result. So when there is revenue for the current time period, the DIVIDE function divides the result of the subtraction of [Sum of Revenue PreviousYear] from [Sum of Revenue] by [Sum of Revenue PreviousYear].

Data Model Tip: The DIVIDE Function

The DIVIDE function ensures that either BLANK or an actual value is returned and is optimized for performance. When you use the / operator, DAX has to handle the divide-by-zero error every time it happens, and this results in a performance hit. The DIVIDE function is short-circuited to just return BLANK or an error value that you can optionally enter in the arguments when a divide-by-zero error is encountered. It's recommended to use the DIVIDE function whenever possible.

Because this is a percentage, Jim changes the format to percentage, and he adds the measure to the matrix.

Region	Sum of Revenue	Revenue to target	Sum of Revenue YoY%
CENTRAL	$176,989.31	$22,984.06	42.64%
EAST	$621,381.14	$113,519.76	23.51%
NORTH	$437,551.91	$46,011.37	400.45%
SOUTH	$178,088.65	$41,858.61	1106.87%
WEST	$426,652.55	$77,610.50	-52.28%

Figure 4.22: The measure is added to a matrix.

Jim has created all the calculations needed for the regions view. He doesn't like the titles of the headers, so he changes them in the matrix. To do so, he double-clicks the name of a column in the Values area and types a new label. Measures usually have very long names, and using them as is results in a lot of unused whitespace in a visual. Renaming the labels to make them shorter allows Jim to get rid of this whitespace and make the visual more understandable for the end users.

Figure 4.23: Renaming column labels.

Next, Jim sets the alignment of the column headers to center alignment in the Format pane.

Jim usually customizes the formatting at the visual level, but in this case he just wants to change the default decimal places to zero because on such large numbers, extra decimal places don't add much value but take up a lot of space and make the numbers harder to read. On the Format pane, in the Field Formatting section, for each field he sets Value Decimal Places to 0.

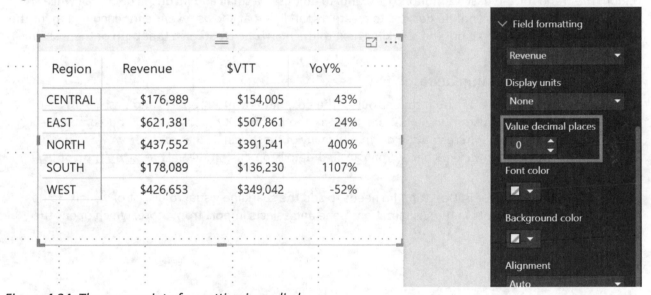

Figure 4.24: The appropriate formatting is applied.

Visualization Tip: Choosing the Right Precision

Here's another opportunity to make your information easier to digest: Determine what level of precision you need for the values you show. Dashboards usually present information at a very high level. Does it really make a difference if you show two decimal places? Or can you get rid of them? $45,223.12 and $45,223 tell the same story when you're talking about the revenue of an entire company. Of course, you should use your best judgment and not remove too much information. For example, in service-level agreements (SLAs), the difference between 99.34% and 99.96% is likely to be crucial, so you should keep the decimal places.

Changing the precision is easy to do, and you'll be surprised how much improvement this simple step will gain you.

One of the things Jim has learned over the years is that it is important to make sure a matrix will not change layout whenever changes are made to the sheet, which would ruin the layout he has so painstakingly crafted. He therefore selects the matrix and turns off Auto-Size Column Width under Column Headers in the Format pane.

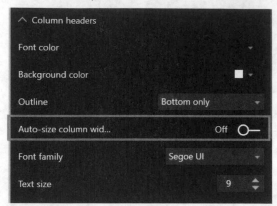

Figure 4.25: Disabling Auto-Size Column Width for columns in a matrix prevents hassle later on.

In Jim's interviews with the board members, he learned that in addition to the information for each region for the current month, they also want to be able to see the trend. Jim therefore wants to show, for each region, the trend for the past 12 months. He wants to do this in a small and inconspicuous way while still managing to convey the trend. He decides to create a sparkline that shows revenue for each region for the past 12 months. He wants to put the sparkline next to the matrix he created so that both of them show data for the same regions.

Power BI Tip: Using Custom Visuals

Power BI contains many visualizations out of the box, but Power BI reports and dashboards can be extended with custom visualizations built by the community or by specialized companies. Power BI has a store where you can download many of these visuals that range from word clouds to Gantt charts and Mekko charts. You can find details on custom visuals at **http://ppivot.us/ chixf32f**.

To add a sparkline in Power BI Desktop, Jim needs to add the sparkline visual to his list of visuals. To do this, he clicks the three dots in the Visualizations pane and selects Import from Store, which opens the custom visuals store.

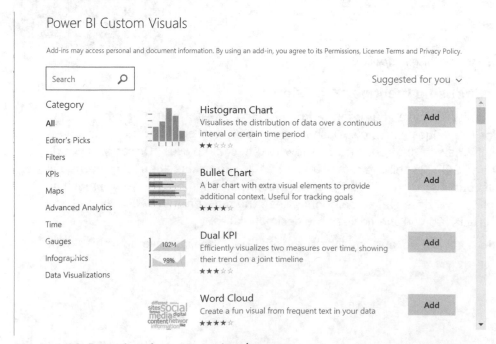

Figure 4.26: Browsing the custom visuals store.

Jim finds the sparkline visual and clicks Add next to it. The custom visual is added to his list of available visualizations.

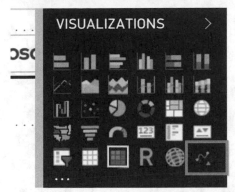

Figure 4.27: The custom visual is added to the Visualizations pane.

Jim now drags the sparkline visualization onto the canvas, and because he wants to see the sales over the past 12 months, he drags YearMonth to the Axis area and Region to the Category area.

To make sure just data from the past 12 months appears, counting back from the last month for which he has data, Jim can use the previously created calculated column Running 12 FY Months, which returns 1 for each day in the past 12 months that has data. He adds this column under Visual Level Filters to automatically select the past 12 months for which he has data.

Next, Jim adds the measure [Revenue to Target] to the matrix to get values for revenue variance-to-target for the past 12 months for which there is data. He now has the sparkline he wants.

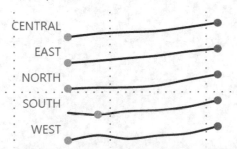

Figure 4.28: Revenue variance-to-target for the past 12 months.

Visualization Tip: Understanding Sparklines

Professor Edward Tufte introduced the sparkline in his book *Beautiful Evidence* (**http://ppivot.us/ fgsd3fd**). He said, "A sparkline is a small, intense, simple, word-sized graphic with typographic resolution. Sparklines mean that graphics are no longer cartoonish special occasions with captions and boxes, but rather sparkline graphics can be everywhere a word or number can be: embedded in a sentence, table, headline, map, spreadsheet, graphic."

Tufte invented the sparkline as a graphic that shows a trend in a space where you would usually have a label or text. A simple graphic shows trends much more clearly than does a range of numbers. Sparklines also save space on reports.

There are three main types of sparklines:

- **Line:** A line sparkline is usually used for chronological time series and other sequence values on the axis, such as stages of a production process. Line sparklines are very useful in helping spot changes or trends in data over time. This is the type Jim is using in Power BI.

- **Column:** A column sparkline is usually used to compare amounts between specific discrete categorical values.

- **Win/loss:** A win/loss sparkline is a special form of sparkline that shows whether data is positive (such as a win) or negative (such as a loss). This type of sparkline is great for showing stock tickers.

For more information, see the extensive Q&A on sparklines on Edward Tufte's website: **http://ppivot.us/ZBPHS**. For more examples of sparklines in Excel, see this great article full of examples from Bill Jelen: **http://ppivot.us/GSEVU**.

Jim moves the matrix to the right to create space for the sparkline and then moves the sparkline to the left of the matrix. To save space, Jim turns off the category labels in the Format pane because the same labels are also present in the matrix.

	Region	Revenue	$VTT	YoY%
	CENTRAL	$176,989	$22,984	43%
	EAST	$621,381	$113,520	24%
	NORTH	$437,552	$46,011	400%
	SOUTH	$178,089	$41,859	1107%
	WEST	$426,653	$77,611	-52%

Figure 4.29: Sparklines moved into position.

Jim uses a text box to add the title $VTT 12 Months to the column that contains the sparklines. This great visual allows Jim to show the trend for each region over the past 12 months.

$VTT 12 Months	Region	Revenue	$VTT	YoY%
	CENTRAL	$176,989	$22,984	43%
	EAST	$621,381	$113,520	24%
	NORTH	$437,552	$46,011	400%
	SOUTH	$178,089	$41,859	1107%
	WEST	$426,653	$77,611	-52%

Figure 4.30: Sparklines applied to the report.

From the dashboard that Jim has created, it's pretty clear that the targets have been met for all regions. Interestingly, the west region was the weakest growth area. Maybe the target was not aggressive enough. The information provided by the dashboard will definitely provide enough material to generate some discussion in the next management meeting.

The next report Jim wants to tackle is one to help gain insight into whether the marketing efforts in new markets have resulted in increased revenue in those markets. Each region was responsible for its own marketing, and the board will want to see this information split out by region.

Jim decides to use a graph, split out by region, to present the number of markets for which there have been sales over the past 12 months.

Visualization Tip: Choosing the Right Chart

Choosing the right chart to show data might be the most difficult problem in data visualization. Unfortunately, there is no surefire way to choose the right chart. Which one is best depends on many, many factors—and on the data you want to show. You have to think about what information you want to show and what information is important. The core idea behind graphs and charts is that they help people understand data quickly and allow you to tell the story behind the data. Therefore, an important factor in choosing and designing the right chart is having a good understanding of the data and the types of charts.

There are four basic types of chart visualizations: those that make a comparison between data points, those that show the distribution of data points, those that show the relationships between data points, and those that show how data points are put together (composition). These visualizations help your audience see what you are talking about.

Let's look at an example for each type:

- **Comparison:** You use this type of chart when you want to compare two or more data points, such as the revenue for each month between years, revenue by region, or revenue for each month for the current year. This is the most common type and is usually a line, bar, or column chart.

- **Distribution:** This is the second most common chart category. As the name suggests, a distribution chart is used to display how data is distributed and to understand outliers and categories that are outside the norm (for example, distribution of voters per region, types of returned products over the past month).

- **Relationship:** This type of chart shows interesting relationships that can lead to new understanding about correlations and causality between a wide range of variables. For example, you might use this type of chart if you want to prove whether hours of study make for better results or to show the relationship between in-store sales and holidays. The most common relationship charts are scatter plots and bubble charts.

- **Composition:** This type of chart allows you to display how specific data compares to broader data (for example, what browser types are visiting a website, product sales as a percentage of total revenue). Commonly used composition charts are column charts, bar charts, and pie charts.

When I'm trying to choose the right chart, I often use this graphic created by Andrew Abela: **http://ppivot.us/TPXGX**.

Jim adds a line chart to the report, directly besides the regions matrix he just created. Next, he adds FyYearLabel and FyMonthLabel under Axis, Region under Legend, and Running 12 FY Months under Filters (to return only the past 12 months).

Jim then adds a measure for counting the number of distinct cities that have revenue. In the Invoice table, every Contoso Communications sales transaction creates a new row. Every row in the Transaction table contains a reference to where the transaction happened, and this information is stored in the PoliticalGeographyKey column. Here is Jim's measure for distinctly counting the markets:

```
[Nr of markets] =
    DISTINCTCOUNT(Invoice[PoliticalGeographyKey])
```

The DISTINCTCOUNT function counts the distinct number of occurrences for each value of PoliticalGeographyKey column in the Invoice table.

Data Model Tip: Remembering That Context Is Always Applied

As mention in Chapter 3, it's important to remember the context in which a calculation will be executed. The expression above will always calculate DISTINCTCOUNT for Invoice[PoliticalGeographyKey] for the values in that cell, filtered by what is on Rows, Columns, Filters, and Slicers. Whether you put regions, years, or products on Rows, the value of DISTINCTCOUNT for Invoice[PoliticalGeographyKey] will automatically be calculated for the values that determine the context.

Adding this measure to the line chart gives Jim almost the chart he wants. However, right now the chart is sorted in descending order, which means the last year appears first. To fix this, he clicks on the three dots in the upper-right corner and selects the ascending sort order. Figure 4.31 shows the resulting chart.

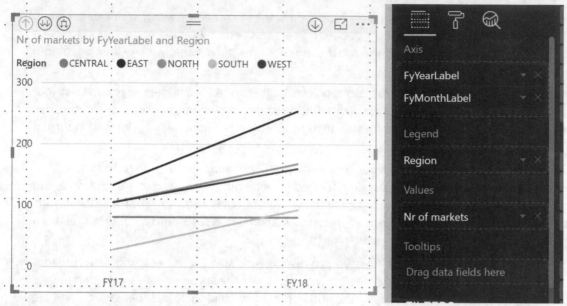

Figure 4.31: Adding values to the chart.

Jim is not satisfied yet because he wants to see the months and years in the chart. To fix this, he clicks the expand icon on the chart's top bar and then expands the values of the chart over both values of the axis by drilling down. This still doesn't give him what he wants because the values are repeated for each month. To change this, he turns off the Concatenate Labels option for the x-axis in the Format pane.

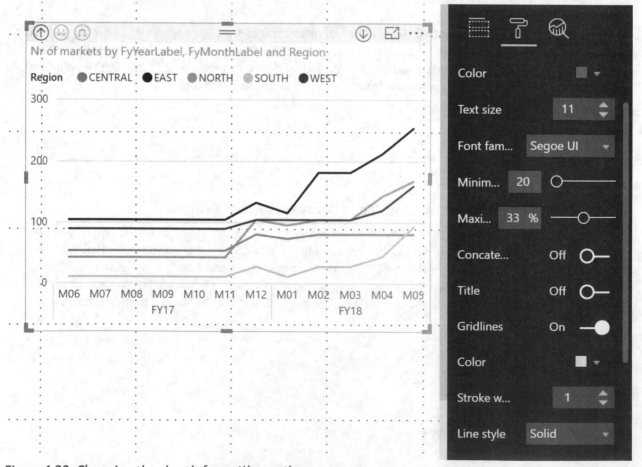

Figure 4.32: Changing the chart's formatting options.

Now Jim wants to align this chart perfectly with the matrix, so he ensures that the chart automatically snaps to the gridlines when it's placed on the grid. Next, he turns off the title. Finally, he makes the chart a little wider on the x-axis and smaller on the y-axis. Jim now has a clear chart of the market growth over the past 12 months.

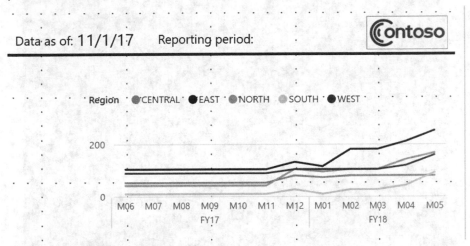

Figure 4.33: The finished chart.

Jim looks for feedback on the first iteration of the dashboard from several business users who will be using the report. The feedback he gets is overwhelmingly positive, but one remark he hears multiple times is that the users wish they could see the report show either the current month, quarter-to-date (QTD), or year-to-date (YTD). Jim agrees that this would be a great addition to the report, and he knows that slicers can help him achieve it. Users will be able to select whatever time period they want to see.

To create slicers, he needs to have data to show, so Jim clicks Enter Data on the Home tab and enters the values he wants: Actual, QTD, and YTD. He names the table varPeriod and the column Period.

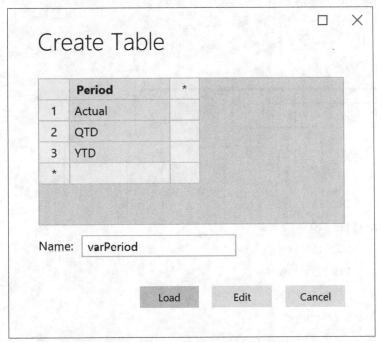

Figure 4.34: Adding new values to a new table.

After Jim clicks Load, these values are added to a new table in the model.

Jim can now use this data to create a slicer. He selects the visuals on the screen and drags them down. Next, he inserts a slicer visual and adds the Period column he just created.

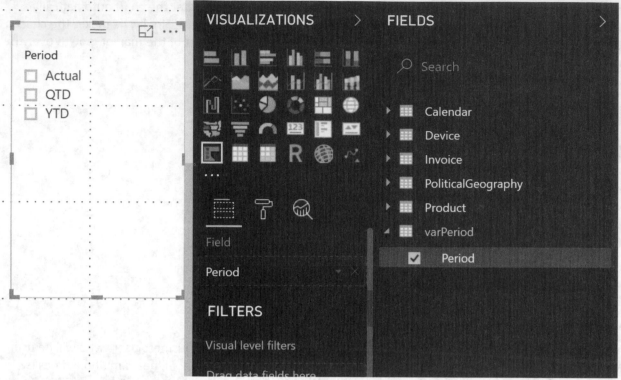

Figure 4.35: Adding values to a slicer.

Jim changes the orientation to Horizontal in the Format pane of the slicer under General. This makes the slicer values sit next to each other instead of one above the other. Next, he turns off the header and adds an outline for the items of the type frame. He matches the color of the outline with the color used as the matrix line. Finally, he arranges the slicer above the matrix.

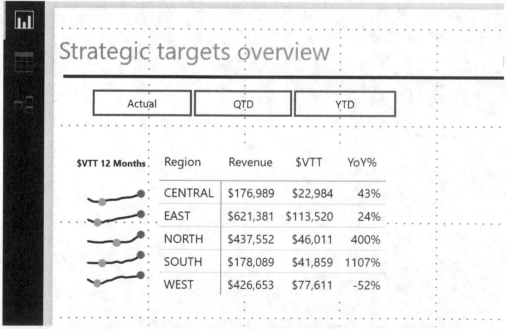

Figure 4.36: The slicer is added to the report.

To make sure the users of the report cannot select multiple values at the same time, Jim turns on Single Select under the selection controls on the Format pane.

Based on the slicer selection, Jim wants to show the actual, fiscal quarter-to-date, or fiscal year-to-date value for each calculation. Jim already has the values for actual, and he decides to add separate measures for fiscal QTD and fiscal YTD.

He adds a measure that determines the fiscal year-to-date sum of revenue:

```
[Sum of Revenue F YTD]=
 IF(HASONEVALUE(Calendar[FyYear]),
     TOTALYTD([Sum of Revenue]
             ,Calendar[Date]
             ,"06/30")
    )
```

> This calculation uses the [Sum of Revenue] measure for the entire YTD. In this case, "to date" is based on the last date in the cell for which this measure is executed. The year is defined as ending on June 30, making this work for a fiscal YTD. To make sure the calculation provides the right information per year, HASONEVALUE makes sure this calculation returns values only when there is only one DateTable[FyYear] selected.

Next, Jim creates a measure that uses Sum of Revenue F YTD to determine the fiscal year-to-date sum for the previous year:

```
[Sum of Revenue F YTD PreviousYear]=
 IF(HASONEVALUE(Calendar[FyYear]),
     CALCULATE([Sum of Revenue F YTD]
             ,DATEADD(Calendar[Date]
                    , -1
                    , YEAR)
            )
    )
```

> This calculation finds the Sum of Revenue F YTD for the entire YTD. But instead of using the date of the cell in the visual, DATEADD moves this date back one year from the dates in the current cell selection.

Jim then creates a measure that determines the year-over-year growth by subtracting the revenue for the current fiscal YTD from the revenue for the previous fiscal YTD and divides the result by the revenue for the previous fiscal YTD—but only when there is revenue for the current year:

```
[Sum of Revenue F YTD YoY%]=
 IF(NOT(ISBLANK([Sum of Revenue])),
     DIVIDE([Sum of Revenue F YTD]
            - [Sum of Revenue F YTD PreviousYear]
           ,[Sum of Revenue F YTD PreviousYear])
    )
```

> The DIVIDE function is used to make sure divide-by-zero errors will not be thrown. Instead, when these errors occur, blank values will be returned.

Jim now uses the same technique to calculate the fiscal year-to-date sum of revenue target:

```
[Sum of RevenueTarget F YTD]=
 IF(HASONEVALUE('Calendar'[FyYear]),
     TOTALYTD([Sum of RevenueTarget],
             'Calendar'[Date]
             ,"06/30")
    )
```

Finally, he creates a measure to calculate the revenue variance-to-target for the fiscal year by subtracting [Sum of RevenueTarget F YTD] from [Sum of Revenue F YTD]:

```
[Revenue to target F YTD]=
 [Sum of Revenue F YTD]-[Sum of RevenueTarget F YTD]
```

Jim creates the same calculation for fiscal quarter-to-date:

```
[Sum of Revenue F QTD] =
 IF(HASONEVALUE(Calendar[FYQuarter]),
    TOTALQTD([Sum of Revenue]
            ,Calendar[Date])
    )
```

> Because fiscal quarters usually don't run differently from normal quarters, this calculation can use the TOTALQTD function.

To calculate Revenue to Target F QTD and Sum of Revenue F QTD YoY%, Jim uses the same calculation pattern as for the YTD measures but replaces the [Sum of Revenue F YTD] measure for [Sum of Revenue F QTD].

After Jim has added measures to calculate revenue, variance-to-target, and year-over-year growth for the current month, fiscal QTD, and fiscal YTD, he needs to find a way to make the values on his report respect the slicer he just created. Jim therefore creates a measure that he can reference in all other measures to check whether the slicer has only one value selected. He doesn't want to show any value when the user selects both YTD and QTD. He creates the following measure to check whether the slicer has only one value selected:

```
[isReportSlicerSet]=
 HASONEVALUE(varPeriod[Period])
```

> This measure uses the HASONEVALUE function to return true or false, depending on whether varPeriod[Period] has one value for the current cell where the calculation field is executed in the visual.

Before he continues, Jim hides the measure because he doesn't need it in anything except as a building block in other measures.

Jim next creates the following measure to return a result based on the value of the slicer:

```
RevenueByPeriod =
 IF([isReportSlicerSet],
    SWITCH(VALUES(varPeriod[Period]),
        "Actual",[Sum of Revenue],
        "YTD",[Sum of Revenue F YTD],
        "QTD",[Sum of Revenue F QTD]
        )
    )
```

> When the [isReportSlicerSet] measure returns true, the VALUES function determines the current value for varPeriod[Period] for this visual. If you didn't check for the single value of varPeriod[Period] and the user selected multiple values in the slicer, the VALUES function would return an error because it wouldn't return a single value. The SWITCH statement then determines which measure will be executed, based on the value of varPeriod[Period].

Data Model Tip: The VALUES Function

The VALUES function allows you to use values in the current context of the visual. Consider the follow DAX formula:

```
[Test Value]=
            IF(HASONEVALUE(PoliticalGeography[Region]) &&
                HASONEVALUE(Calendar[FyYearLabel]),
                    VALUES(PoliticalGeography[Region]) &
                    " " &
                    VALUES(Calendar[FyYearLabel]))
```

This formula shows the value of PoliticalGeography[Region] and Calendar[FyYearLabel] in each cell in the matrix where the cell has only one value for each.

FyYearLabel	CENTRAL	EAST	NORTH	SOUTH	WEST	Total
FY14	CENTRAL FY14	EAST FY14	NORTH FY14	SOUTH FY14	WEST FY14	
FY15	CENTRAL FY15	EAST FY15	NORTH FY15	SOUTH FY15	WEST FY15	
FY16	CENTRAL FY16	EAST FY16	NORTH FY16	SOUTH FY16	WEST FY16	
FY17	CENTRAL FY17	EAST FY17	NORTH FY17	SOUTH FY17	WEST FY17	
FY18	CENTRAL FY18	EAST FY18	NORTH FY18	SOUTH FY18	WEST FY18	
FY19	CENTRAL FY19	EAST FY19	NORTH FY19	SOUTH FY19	WEST FY19	
Total						

Figure 4.37: The VALUES function is used to show the context.

You can use the VALUES function in many situations, such as in a running sum, where you use it to get the current month to determine the time range for a calculation.

Jim repeats the same pattern for variation-to-target and year-over-year revenue.

You can download a file that contains all the measures used until Figure 4.47 from **http://ppivot. us/daxm231**. You can also download a text file that has all the measures for this part of the chapter from **http://ppivot.us/filmea2s**. The following measures are small variations of the measures just created so are not really interesting to cover in detail here.

Next, Jim replaces the measures from the matrix with the newly created measures. He also sets the same formatting and applies the same header names.

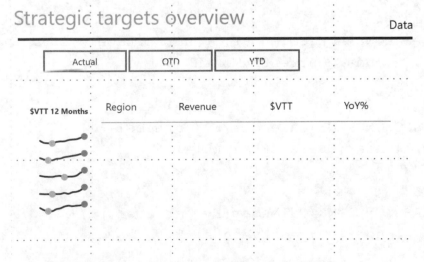

Figure 4.38: The new measures are added to the report.

The measures are empty, as expected, so Jim clicks the YTD slicer, and now the measures show the values he expects.

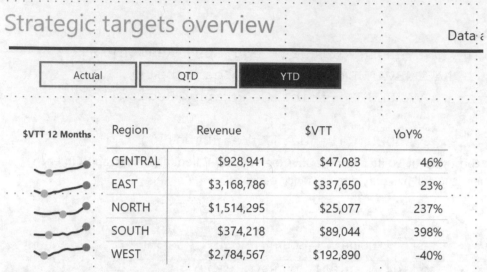

$VTT 12 Months	Region	Revenue	$VTT	YoY%
	CENTRAL	$928,941	$47,083	46%
	EAST	$3,168,786	$337,650	23%
	NORTH	$1,514,295	$25,077	237%
	SOUTH	$374,218	$89,044	398%
	WEST	$2,784,567	$192,890	-40%

Figure 4.39: Values in the matrix now show up.

Jim also wants to hook up the Reporting Period: title to the slicer to report the right reporting period for each slicer. To make this happen, he adds the following new measure, which checks the selection and generates a title on demand:

```
Reporting Period =
 IF(HASONEVALUE(varPeriod[Period]),
    SWITCH(VALUES(varPeriod[Period])
    ,"Actual",
        CALCULATE(
                LASTNONBLANK(Calendar[FYMonthLabel],1)
                ,Calendar[CurrentFyMonth]=1)
        & " " &
        CALCULATE(
                LASTNONBLANK(Calendar[FyYearLabel],1)
                ,Calendar[CurrentFyMonth]=1)
                ,"QTD",
        CALCULATE(
                LASTNONBLANK(Calendar[FyQuarterLabel],1)
                ,Calendar[CurrentFyMonth]=1)
        & " " &
        CALCULATE(
                LASTNONBLANK(Calendar[FyYearLabel],1)
                ,Calendar[CurrentFyMonth]=1)
                ,"YTD",
        CALCULATE(
                LASTNONBLANK(Calendar[FyYearLabel],1)
                ,Calendar[CurrentFyMonth]=1)
    )
 , "N/A")
```

> I chose to use to use HASONEVALUE here instead of using SELECTEDVALUE as I want to have the measure return N/A when nothing can be returned.

Now Jim adds this measure to a card visual, turns off the category label, and changes the text to size 11 and font Segoe UI. Placing the card visual next to the Reporting Period: label gives him what he wants.

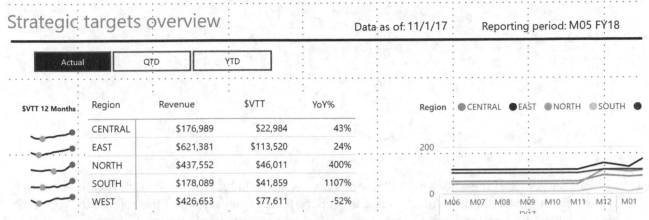

Figure 4.40: The title reacts to slicer clicks.

The next part of the dashboard is really the centerpiece of the report. One of the most important requirements is to be able to see the rhythm of the business for each key metric for the current month, current QTD, and current fiscal YTD. The key metrics of the business are revenue, units, usage, and subscribers. For each of these metrics, Jim needs to show the actuals, variance-to-target, and year-over-year growth for each time period in the report. This report needs to be connected to the slicer he just created.

Jim has been creating these reports for years and knows what to do. He knows that the regular matrix is unable to achieve the type of layout he needs, and he has to use a different approach. He wants the visual to show up at the top of the report, so Jim moves all the visuals down. He makes sure the reports are aligned properly and ensures that they have the same style.

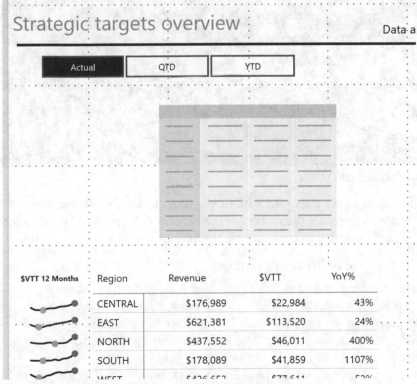

Figure 4.41: Creating the framework for the report.

Jim now wants to add the values of the metrics to the report. He decides to create another table called KeyMetrics to define the metrics, and he does so by clicking the Enter Data button (**http://ppivot.us/ent-data**).

Create Table

	Values	Pos	*
1	Revenue	1	
2	Units	2	
3	Usage	3	
4	Subscribers	4	
*			

Figure 4.42: Adding a new table for the values.

To make sure he can sort the values in the table in any way, Jim includes a position field. The default sorting of any column is alphabetical. After loading the report, Jim sets the sorting of the column to Pos, which causes the values to be sorted by the numbers in the Pos column instead of alphabetically.

Figure 4.43: Changing the sorting of the Values column.

Jim now adds the Values column to the matrix to get the metrics he needs to write another DAX expression. But before he can start on this, he needs to create measures for the Actual, VTT, and YoY% metrics for units, usage, and subscribers, using the same calculation template he created for revenue.

Data Model Tip: Making a Template of Your Measures

You will likely find that you create the same measures over and over, with just small variations, just as Jim did. In his case, Jim used a different base measure, but the rest stayed the same. Keep this in the back of your mind as you design your measures. It is important to split up your measures into smaller calculations and reuse those building blocks wherever possible. Also, make sure to hide the intermediate calculations when you don't think there is going to be a need for them in your visuals. Hidden calculations will not show in the Fields pane, but you will be able to reference them in other calculations.

To make use of the values in the Values column, Jim creates another measure to determine which measure to show in the matrix:

```
[KeyMetricActual] =
 SWITCH(SELECTEDVALUE(Keymetrics[Values])
              ,"Revenue"
              ,FORMAT([RevenueByPeriod], "$#,##0")
              ,"Subscribers"
              ,FORMAT([SubscriberCountByPeriod], "#,##")
              ,"Units"
              ,FORMAT([UnitsByPeriod], "#,##")
              ,"Usage"
              ,FORMAT([UsageByPeriod], "#,##")
         )
```

> This measure uses the SELECTEDVALUE function to get the value of the Values column and then dynamically select the measure to display. SELECTEDVALUE returns NULL when more than a single value is getting returned. This makes it more convenient than using IF (HASONEVALUE (– *Column*), SWITCH (VALUES (*Column*)). By using the FORMAT function, you can format each result differently; in this example, the results for "Revenue" should return currency format, and the rest of the results should be regular numbers.

When Jim adds this measure to the matrix, the values are aligned left. Because Jim used the FORMAT function, the data was returned as text. Using the Field Formatting settings in the Format pane, he changes the alignment to right alignment. To get the sales based on the current period, he adds CurrentFyMonth under Visual Level Filter.

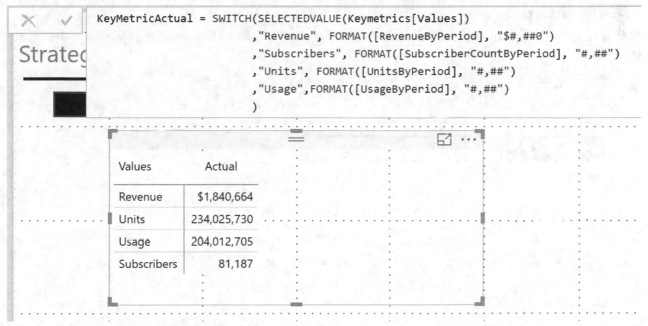

Figure 4.44: Adding the special measure.

Next, Jim changes the measure name to Actual and adds a new measure for the variance-to-target values:

```
[KeyMetricVTT] =
        SWITCH(SELECTEDVALUE(Keymetrics[Values])
                ,"Revenue"
                ,FORMAT([RevenueToTargetByPeriod], "$#,##0")
                ,"Subscribers"
                ,"n/a"
                ,"Units"
                ,FORMAT([UnitsToTargetByPeriod], "#,##")
                ,"Usage"
                ,FORMAT([UsageToTargetByPeriod], "#,##")
            )
```

Because the company doesn't have any targets for subscribers, Jim enters n/a for not available under VTT for Subscribers. He also changes the field formatting to be aligned right.

Finally, Jim creates this measure for YoY%:

```
[KeyMetricYoY] =
        SWITCH(SELECTEDVALUE(Keymetrics[Values])
                ,"Revenue", [RevenueYoYByPeriod]
                ,"Subscribers", [SubscriberCountYoYByPeriod]
                ,"Units", [UnitsYoYByPeriod]
                ,"Usage",[UsageYoYByPeriod])
```

Here, because everything is a percentage, Jim doesn't have to use the Format function, but he uses the default format that is set on the measure.

Putting together these measures gives Jim a matrix that show all values that react to selection in the slicer above it.

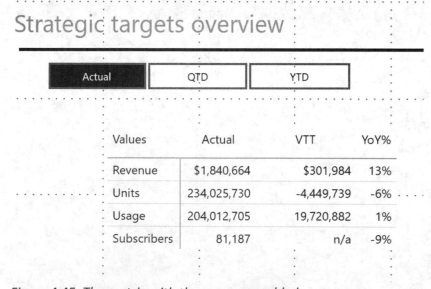

Values	Actual	VTT	YoY%
Revenue	$1,840,664	$301,984	13%
Units	234,025,730	-4,449,739	-6%
Usage	204,012,705	19,720,882	1%
Subscribers	81,187	n/a	-9%

Figure 4.45: The matrix with the measures added.

Jim also wants to show the trend for each of the metrics for the past 12 months, so he creates another sparkline. To do this, he creates a similar measure to display the value for each type:

```
[KeyMetricSparkline] =
    SWITCH(SELECTEDVALUE(Keymetrics[Values])
```

```
        ,"Revenue", [Sum of Revenue]
        ,"Subscribers", [Sum of SubscriberCount]
        ,"Units", [Sum of Units]
        ,"Usage", [Sum of Usage])
```

He then adds the same sparkline visual to the report. Jim also adds Running 12 Months under Filter and the new [KeyMetricSparkline] measure under Values. Finally, he adds YearMonth under Axis Columns and turns off the category label.

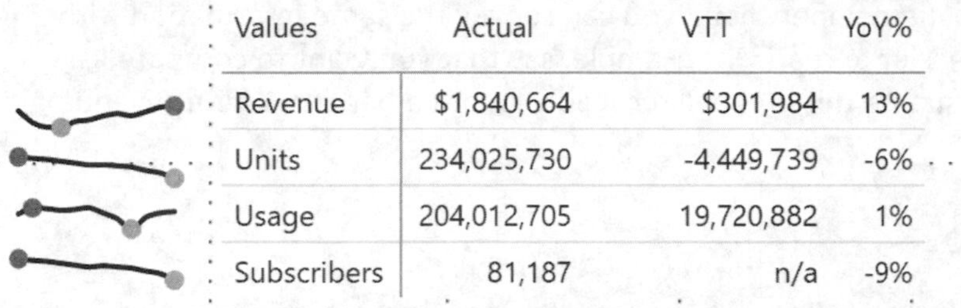

Values	Actual	VTT	YoY%
Revenue	$1,840,664	$301,984	13%
Units	234,025,730	-4,449,739	-6%
Usage	204,012,705	19,720,882	1%
Subscribers	81,187	n/a	-9%

Figure 4.46: The sparkline added to the report.

Jim also adds the title Last 12 Months above the matrix, and then, noticing that the two matrixes are not aligned, he spends some time aligning and working on synchronizing their formatting until he gets the desired result. He also makes sure he maximizes the space for the sparklines.

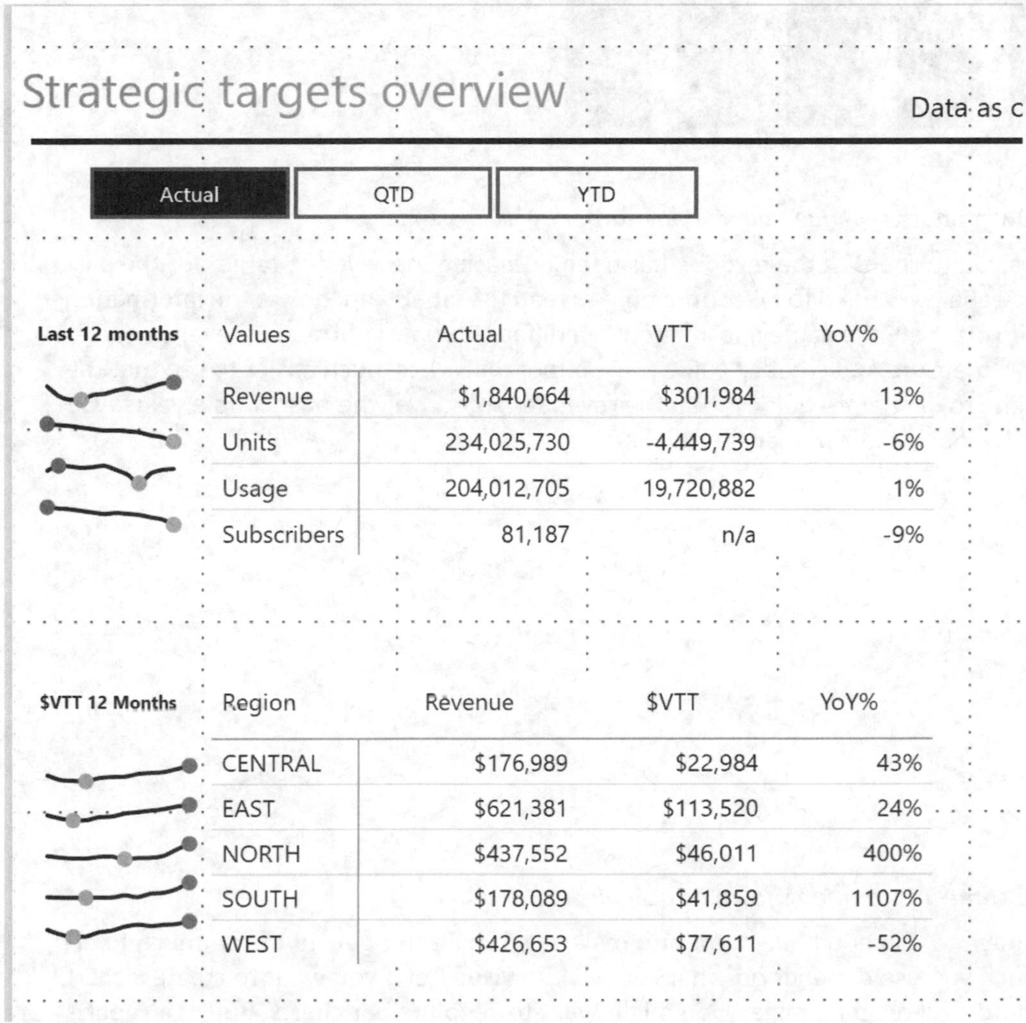

Strategic targets overview
Data as c

Actual	QTD	YTD

Last 12 months	Values	Actual	VTT	YoY%
	Revenue	$1,840,664	$301,984	13%
	Units	234,025,730	-4,449,739	-6%
	Usage	204,012,705	19,720,882	1%
	Subscribers	81,187	n/a	-9%

$VTT 12 Months	Region	Revenue	$VTT	YoY%
	CENTRAL	$176,989	$22,984	43%
	EAST	$621,381	$113,520	24%
	NORTH	$437,552	$46,011	400%
	SOUTH	$178,089	$41,859	1107%
	WEST	$426,653	$77,611	-52%

Figure 4.47: After aligning the visuals.

Jim wants to make the revenue over the past 12 months even more pronounced in the report. To accomplish this, he's going to add a new chart that shows $VTT over the past 12 months. He adds a line chart to the right of the matrix he just created and aligns the two by selecting them both and using the Align tools on the Format pane to align to the top. Then he also makes sure it is aligned to the already existing chart below.

Visualization Tip: Choosing the Right Calculation

Another tip that will help you make your reports more readable is to take a good look at the calculations you use in your charts. Remember that if you can convey the same information with fewer visuals, your report will be easier to read. For example, say that you want to compare values with targets. If you want to visualize this, you will probably create a bar chart with revenue and revenue target by fiscal year.

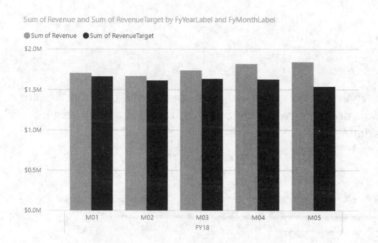

Figure 4.48: Showing both revenue and revenue target by fiscal year.

This chart allows you to see that the revenue has been outpacing the revenue target for the past couple years. However, you need to take some time to read the labels and look at the information up close. Now, if you show the same information in a different way—subtracting revenue target from revenue in a measure and creating a line chart out of that—it is much easier to see that the revenue has been growing more quickly than the revenue target over the past couple years; you can see this just by looking at the shape of the line.

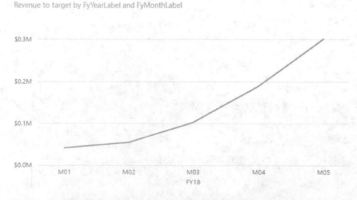

Figure 4.49: The same information shown as a single line.

Of course, you have to use good judgment and make sure you don't get rid of too much information. How much you use depends on what you want to visualize. If you want to create a chart that shows revenue and revenue target, you might want to keep the bar charts. But if the goal is to show revenue compared to revenue target, the single line is much clearer—although it doesn't allow you to see how much revenue was made.

Jim adds Revenue to Target under Values, FyYearLabel and FyMonthLabel under Axis, and Running 12 Months under Visual Level Filters. He sets the filter to 1 and adds the revenue to the target measure. He turns off Concatenate Labels under X-Axis, and he also turns off the title. Finally, Jim makes sure the sorting of the visual is set to ascending.

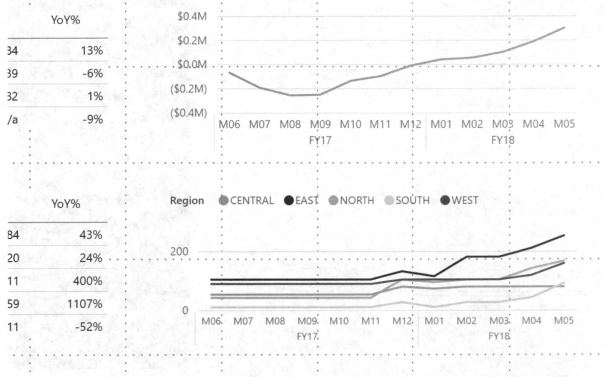

Figure 4.50: The initial chart is created.

Next, Jim wants to change the format of the axis. By default, the Display value is set to Millions, but Jim wants a bit more granularity, so he sets it to Thousands.

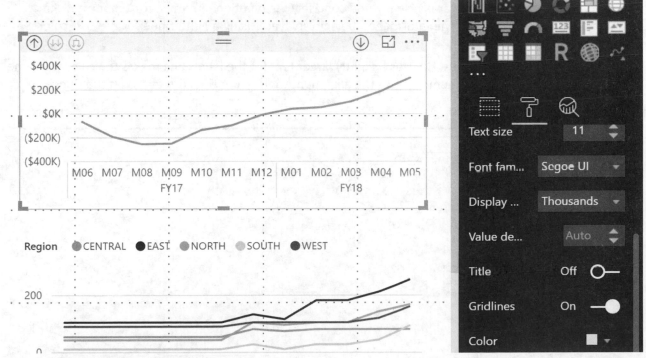

Figure 4.51: Setting the chart axis format.

Jim also wants the user to be able to clearly see whether sales are above or below target, so he adds a new constant line to the chart. He goes to the Analytics pane and adds a constant line with Color set to red, Value set to 0, and Line Style set to Dotted.

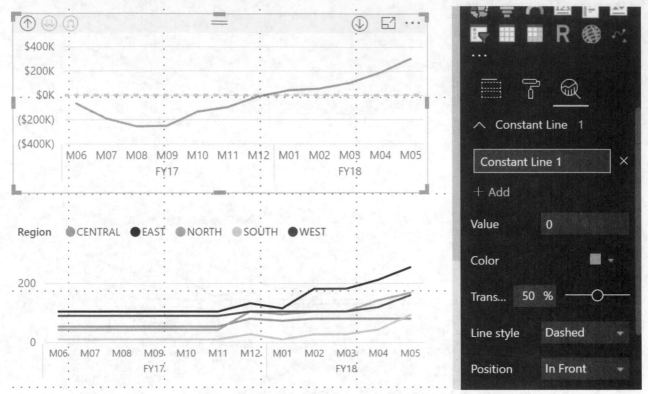

Figure 4.52: The dotted line clearly shows what is above and what is below the target.

Visualization Tip: Labeling Appropriately

In order for a user to differentiate the various reports onscreen, you need to provide appropriate information and label the areas clearly and concisely. As mentioned earlier, it is important that a label not compete with the information being displayed. Using a lighter hue for the text color helps with this.

Jim now adds labels to his visuals. He uses a slightly larger font for the labels and makes the color the same as for the report title. To align them, he uses the alignment tools under the Format tab on the ribbon.

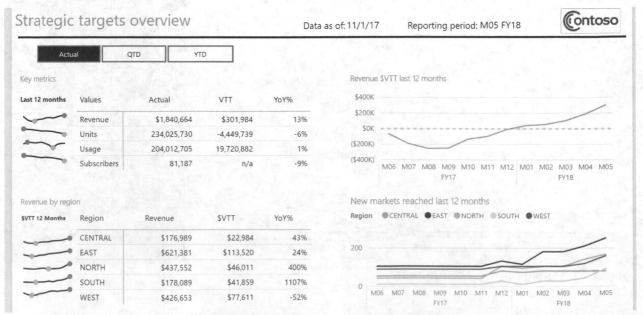

Figure 4.53: The dashboard with labels added.

One of the marketing teams has been working on promoting the top-selling products. Jim wants to create a table that shows the sales for the 10 best-selling products by revenue, their percentage of the total, and their percentage year-over-year growth.

Jim copies the regions matrix in order to automatically get all the same settings on the new matrix. In the new copy, he replaces Region on Rows with DeviceName, and he removes the [$VTT] and [YoY%] measures; however, he can reuse the [Revenue] measure. He notices that DeviceName takes up a bit more space than Region did, so he rearranges all three matrix visuals a bit to make them even again.

Revenue by region

Region	Revenue	$VTT	YoY%
CENTRAL	$176,989	$22,984	43%
EAST	$621,381	$113,520	24%
NORTH	$437,552	$46,011	400%
SOUTH	$178,089	$41,859	1107%
WEST	$426,653	$77,611	-52%

$VTT 12 Months

DeviceName	Revenue
Aircard 1	$36
Aircard 2	$9
Aircard 3	$24,845
Aircard 4	$25,288
Cable Modem 1	$15,398
Cable Modem 10	$44,742
Cable Modem 11	$73,552
Cable Modem 2	$15,619
Cable Modem 3	$15,985

Figure 4.54: A visual for devices and revenue.

To get the top 10 devices by revenue, Jim uses the native filtering and ordering. He clicks the arrow at the row header to sort in descending order. To show only the top 10, he can add a special filter at the DeviceName field under Visual Levels Filter that he can configure to show the top 10 based on the [RevenueByPeriod] measure. Jim now sees just 10 products in the visual instead of the entire list.

DeviceName	Revenue
Video Stream	$141,718
Mobile1015	$140,115
Mobile1014	$138,163
Mobile1018	$84,835
Cable Modem 11	$73,552
Mobile1017	$70,826
Mobile1016	$69,679
Premium Phone	$55,177
Cable Modem 10	$44,742
MT 1010	$42,645

Revenue

FILTERS

Visual level filters

CurrentFyMonth
is 1

DeviceName
top 10 by RevenueBy...

Revenue (All)

Page level filters

Figure 4.55: Sorting and filtering the data.

Next, Jim adds year-over-year growth by simply adding the [RevenueYoYByPeriod] measure to the matrix.

DeviceName	Revenue	YoY%
Video Stream	$141,718	12%
Mobile1015	$140,115	166%
Mobile1014	$138,163	156%
Mobile1018	$84,835	7%
Cable Modem 11	$73,552	1%
Mobile1017	$70,826	12%
Mobile1016	$69,679	5%
Premium Phone	$55,177	1%
Cable Modem 10	$44,742	8%
MT 1010	$42,645	-4%

Figure 4.56: The top 10 devices by revenue and YoY%.

Now, for the percentage of total, Jim wants to add a new measure to calculate the revenue for one device compared to the revenue for all devices. Jim adds the following measure to calculate the revenue for all devices:

```
[Revenue all products]=
    CALCULATE([Sum of Revenue],ALL('Product'))
```

This measure determines the sum of revenue for all products, regardless of any filters on Product.

Jim decides that he probably will never use the [Revenue all products] measure directly in his visuals, so he hides it. Now that he has this value, he can divide the sum of revenue for the current product by the revenue for all products:

```
[Pct of all products]=
    DIVIDE([Sum of Revenue], [Revenue all products])
```

This measure divides the sum of revenue for the current product by the revenue for all products.

He then adds the percentage format and sets the number of decimal places to 0. Jim also adds the measure to the visual after the revenue measure. He then makes sure the column headers are Revenue, % to Total, and YoY%. Finally, he adds the label Top 10 Devices by Revenue above the visual. After taking all these steps, Jim sees the results he expects.

Top 10 Devices by Revenue

DeviceName	Revenue	% to total	YoY%
Video Stream	$677,484	8%	5%
Mobile1015	$544,265	8%	119%
Mobile1014	$534,757	8%	110%
Mobile1018	$407,957	5%	-1%
Cable Modem 11	$361,074	4%	-5%
Mobile1017	$338,460	4%	4%
Mobile1016	$335,702	4%	-2%
Premium Phone	$269,727	3%	-3%
Cable Modem 10	$216,553	2%	1%
MT 1010	$209,208	2%	-10%

Figure 4.57: The top 10 devices report.

The visual showing the top 10 devices YTD clearly indicates that some devices have failed to grow substantially, while others have grown astronomically. The board will want to investigate to determine the reasons behind this.

The board had an important request to be able to see whether a cost reduction has had an effect this fiscal year. Jim decides to show this by displaying the revenue per unit compared to the same revenue per unit in the previous year. He decides to show the numbers in a simple line chart.

Jim already created a [Sum of Units] measure, and now he creates a measure that will divide the revenue by the number of units:

```
[Revenue by Units]=
    DIVIDE([Sum of Revenue],[Sum of Units])
```

Next, he wants to get the revenue by units from the previous year, so he creates this measure:

```
[Revenue by Units Previous Year]=
  IF(HASONEVALUE('Calendar'[FyYear]),
    CALCULATE([Revenue by Units],
            SAMEPERIODLASTYEAR('Calendar'[Date])
            )
        )
```

This calculation uses the CALCULATE function to change the date range for the current cell context to the previous year by passing the SAMEPERIODLASTYEAR function as a parameter for CALCULATE. Jim wants to make sure that this measure can be used only when a single year is selected, so he uses the HASONEVALUE function to check whether the current cell really contains only a single year. He now uses SAMEPERIODLASTYEAR instead of DATEADD, but these are actually the same: SAMEPERIODLASTYEAR is just a shorthand notation for ease of use.

Now that Jim has both the revenue by units for the current period and the revenue by units for the previous year, he can calculate the year-over-year growth:

```
[Revenue by Units YoY%]=
IF([Revenue by Units]>0,
        DIVIDE([Revenue by Units]
            -[Revenue by Units Previous Year]
        ,[Revenue by Units Previous Year])
        )
```

Because Jim wants to make sure the percentage will be calculated only when there is revenue by units for the current period, he uses the IF function in the calculation.

Jim also sets the formatting to percentage for this measure. Next, he creates a new chart by copying the Nr of Markets chart that is already on the report. This chart already has the right filter set, so all Jim has to do is remove the region under Legend and the [Nr of Markets] measure under Values and instead insert the [Revenue by Units YoY%] measure.

Jim also adds to this chart the new header Revenue by Unit YoY% Last 12 Months. He finally has a chart that clearly shows that the cost cuts made a difference: Revenue by units was up by over 20%.

Figure 4.58: The chart clearly shows the YoY percentage change over time.

Jim wants to make sure that the board members are able to detect any numbers that they have to take action on.

Visualization Tip: Bringing Attention Where Attention Is Warranted: KPIs

In business intelligence, *KPI* is almost synonymous with *dashboard*. A *KPI*, which stands for *key performance indicator*, is an indicator that is developed to gauge the success or failure of a metric it is associated with. Originally, companies used KPIs to keep track of the key metrics of the business for a period—even before reports and computers became mainstream. In business intelligence, a KPI is usually associated with a visualization such as a traffic light that shows red, green, or yellow to indicate the status of the metric. This visualization is usually a default control or feature in most data visualization tools, including Excel, Power Pivot, and SQL Server Reporting Services.

I usually prefer to abstain from using KPIs, in the traditional BI sense of the word, in my reports and dashboards. Instead, I rely on other visualization methods to bring attention to parts of a dashboard that need the user's immediate attention. When you have an entire dashboard littered with red, green, and yellow colors, it becomes very hard to see anything, and it is difficult to bring attention to a metric that is off target and needs immediate attention. When a metric is on target, does it need to draw attention with a big green icon or green background? Usually the answer is no, but sometimes the answer is yes, depending on the importance of the measure or the business requirements.

Remember that the customer is always boss. Some CFOs or dashboard users expect and want their KPIs to be green when the metrics are on or over target. You should give them what they want if they are not open to other ideas.

Jim selects the key metric matrix again, and on the Format pane he turns on Background Color Scales under Conditional Formatting for the YoY% column.

Figure 4.59: Adding conditional formatting.

This turns on the default setting, but Jim wants to fine-tune it, so he clicks Advanced Controls and checks Color by Rules.

Background color scales

Format cells with color based on their value.

Base value

YoY%

☑ Color by rules

Rules   + Add

| If value | is greater than or equal to ▼ | Minimum | and | is less than ▼ | 0 | then | ▢ ▼ | ↑ ↓ ✕ |

Figure 4.60: Applying the formatting rule.

The report now has dynamic formatting applied to any cell that contains a value below zero.

Key metrics

Last 12 months	Values	Actual	VTT	YoY%
	Revenue	$8,770,807	$691,745	5%
	Units	1,194,362,760	-24,817,276	-5%
	Usage	993,872,639	91,635,628	0%
	Subscribers	419,558	n/a	-7%

Figure 4.61: The report with dynamic formatting applied to YoY%.

Jim adds the same conditional formatting rules to the other YoY% columns of the report. The result is a dashboard that contains all the metrics Jim wants to show.

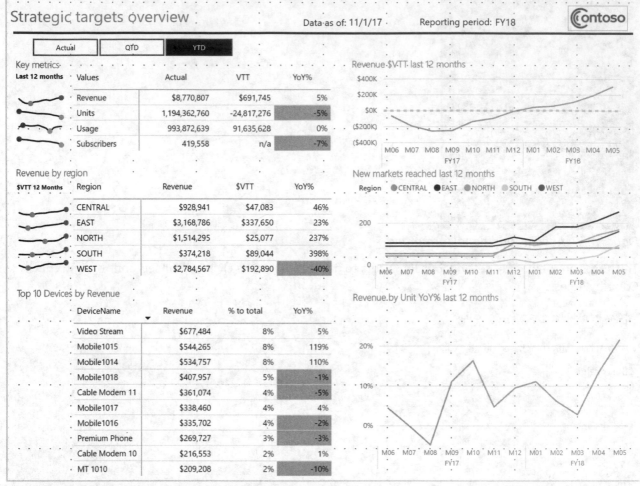

Figure 4.62: All the metrics are added to the dashboard.

Jim is now ready to finish the report and clean it up for the final view. To tidy up, he deselects Show Gridlines. This results in a much cleaner version of the report.

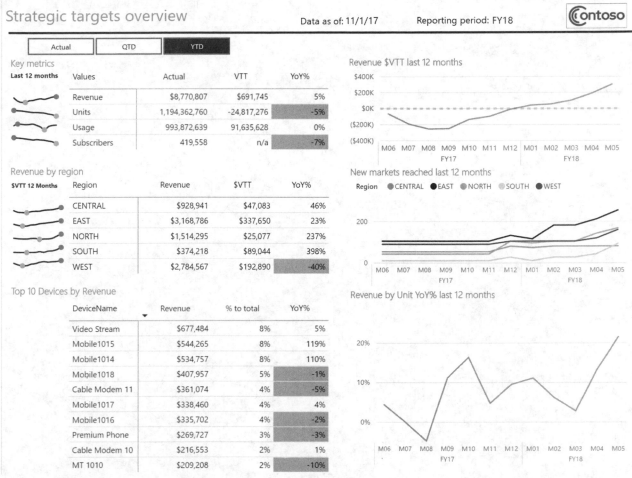

Figure 4.63: Hiding the gridlines.

It's time for Jim to do a last check of the dashboard. He considers the following questions related to factors that make or break a dashboard:

- Are the same fonts used everywhere?
- Do the colors match up?
- Are items that belong together placed together?
- Are the items aligned properly?
- Does the data look correct?
- Do the interactive parts of the dashboard work as expected?

After he has satisfactorily answered all these questions, it's time for Jim to show the dashboard to some of the key users and get their feedback. Then he can do the work needed to allow his users to drill down into more details by creating detailed reports.

5 - Building Detailed Reports

Jim has created the main report, which gives a high-level overview of the data. Now he wants his users to be able to drill down into more details, so they can learn more about what is going on. This chapter walks through the process he follows to create several detailed reports.

Jim thinks he should create a detailed report on revenue. He wants users to be able to use the report to examine revenue information from several angles. They will be able to use what they find in this detailed report to answer many questions raised in the dashboard.

Jim wants to allow users to dive into the following revenue calculations:

- Revenue by region for the current period, QTD, and YTD
- Revenue by region over the current fiscal year
- Revenue by plan type for the current period, QTD, and YTD
- Revenue by plan type over the current fiscal year
- Revenue over time
- Revenue YoY% comparison

Jim knows that this is a lot of data to show, but luckily Power BI allows quite a few tricks to make this amount of data manageable. He opens his Power BI Desktop file and adds a new report, which he calls Revenue. To make the report look consistent with the dashboard, he copies the header from the overview page and changes the title from Strategic Targets Dashboard to Revenue Report.

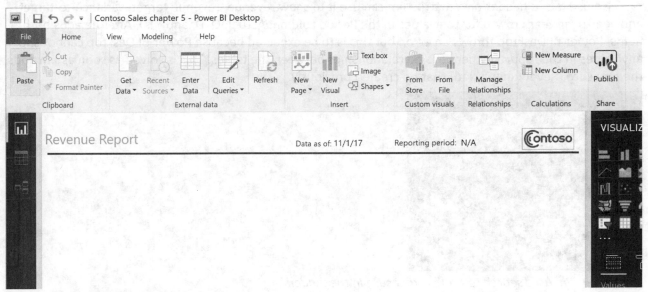

Figure 5.1: Adding a header to a report.

Jim wants to make this report interactive. Instead of having a static reporting period, he wants the user to choose the reporting period. He wants this report to have maximum flexibility, so he chooses to add a slicer that allows the user to select the fiscal year for which to show the data.

Jim adds the FyYearLabel field to the report and clicks on the slicer visual to turn it into a slicer.

Figure 5.2: Turning a field into a slicer.

The current header has a reporting period section where Jim reported on the current reporting period using a static label. Jim wants to replace the static label with the slicer. He decides to turn it into buttons and so goes into the Format pane for the slicer and sets Orientation to Horizontal under General and Outline to Frame under Items to get the result he wants.

Figure 5.3: Making the slicer look like buttons.

He then rearranges the header to put the slicer control buttons where the static label used to appear.

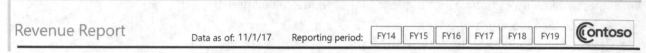

Figure 5.4: Updating the header to add the slicer controls.

To start with a visual that shows detailed revenue by region, Jim adds a matrix that shows regions by various metrics. In this matrix, he turns off Auto-Size Column Width under Column Headers in the Format pane.

To make sure he shows only the sales for the current month, Jim drags the CurrentFyMonth field under Visual Level Filters and selects 1. He then adds the Regions field under Rows and the Period field he created for the dashboard under Columns. In the overview report, Jim used the Report column as a slicer, but he can also use it as a header on a matrix. Jim can use it to show revenue, revenue target, variance-to-target, and year-over-year growth for the values in the Period column: Actual, QTD, and YTD. After he adds both fields, Power BI Desktop throws an error, but this is to be expected because Power BI Desktop cannot show any values in the report as there are no relationships between the tables. This is solved as soon as Jim adds the measure [RevenueByPeriod] that he created previously.

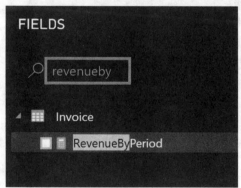

Figure 5.5: Jim uses search to find his measure in the model.

After the measure is added, Jim can see the revenue for the current month, quarter-to-date, and year-to-date for each region.

Revenue Report

Region	Actual	QTD	YTD	Total
CENTRAL	$176,989	$376,494	$928,941	
EAST	$621,381	$1,338,124	$3,168,786	
NORTH	$437,552	$792,711	$1,514,295	
SOUTH	$178,089	$256,821	$374,218	
WEST	$426,653	$893,938	$2,784,567	
Total	**$1,840,664**	**$3,658,088**	**$8,770,807**	

Figure 5.6: Revenue report.

The total for columns doesn't make any sense for this visual, so Jim turns it off under Subtotals in the Format pane.

Jim now needs a measure for revenue target, so he copies the [RevenueByPeriod] measure and creates a new measure called [RevenueToTargetbyPeriod]:

```
[RevenueTargetByPeriod] =
IF([isReportSlicerSet],
    SWITCH(VALUES(varPeriod[Period]) ,
        "Actual",[Sum of RevenueTarget],
        "YTD",[Sum of RevenueTarget F QTD],
        "QTD",[Sum of RevenueTarget F QTD]
        )
    )
```

Jim changes the format of the measure to currency with two decimal places. Finally, he adds the [RevenueTargetByPeriod], [RevenueToTargetByPeriod], and [RevenueYoYByPeriod] measures to the matrix. For each measure, he changes the number of decimal places to zero on the Format pane.

At this point, the matrix shows each result for each time period for each region, along with the grand total.

Period	Actual				QTD		
Region	RevenueByPeriod	RevenueTargetByPeriod	RevenueToTargetByPeriod	RevenueYoYByPeriod	RevenueByPeriod	RevenueTargetByPeriod	RevenueToTarge
CENTRAL	$176,989	$154,005	$22,984	43%	$376,494	$339,635	
EAST	$621,381	$507,861	$113,520	24%	$1,338,124	$1,132,024	
NORTH	$437,552	$391,541	$46,011	400%	$792,711	$726,567	
SOUTH	$178,089	$136,230	$41,859	1107%	$256,821	$191,890	
WEST	$426,653	$349,042	$77,611	-52%	$893,938	$776,118	
Total	**$1,840,664**	**$1,538,679**	**$301,984**	**13%**	**$3,658,088**	**$3,166,234**	

Figure 5.7: Adding the values to the matrix.

Because it's hard to see the entire table, Jim wants to apply some formatting. He starts by renaming the measures to make them more user friendly. He renames all the measures under Values:

- He changes RevenueByPeriod to Actual.
- He changes RevenueTargetByPeriod to Target.
- He changes RevenueToTargetByPeriod to $VTT.
- He changes RevenueYoYByPeriod to YoY%.

To give the matrix a clean and tidy look, Jim applies the matrix style Minimal. He turns off column width auto-sizing and aligns the column headers to the left. Finally, he spaces the columns to remove some of the whitespace. The visual is much easier to read already.

Period	Actual				QTD				YTD			
Region	Actual	Target	$VTT	YoY%	Actual	Target	$VTT	YoY%	Actual	Target	$VTT	YoY%
CENTRAL	$176,989	$154,005	$22,984	43%	$376,494	$339,635	$36,859	47%	$928,941	$339,635	$47,083	46%
EAST	$621,381	$507,861	$113,520	24%	$1,338,124	$1,132,024	$206,100	30%	$3,168,786	$1,132,024	$337,650	23%
NORTH	$437,552	$391,541	$46,011	400%	$792,711	$726,567	$66,144	342%	$1,514,295	$726,567	$25,077	237%
SOUTH	$178,089	$136,230	$41,859	1107%	$256,821	$191,890	$64,931	756%	$374,218	$191,890	$89,044	398%
WEST	$426,653	$349,042	$77,611	-52%	$893,938	$776,118	$117,820	-51%	$2,784,567	$776,118	$192,890	-40%
Total	**$1,840,664**	**$1,538,679**	**$301,984**	**13%**	**$3,658,088**	**$3,166,234**	**$491,854**	**10%**	**$8,770,807**	**$3,166,234**	**$691,745**	**5%**

Figure 5.8: Styling the matrix.

To accentuate the header of the matrix, Jim selects Field Formatting in the Format pane, turns off Apply to Values, and turns on Apply to Header. He then sets the background color to light gray and the alignment to center. He repeats this for each measure. He doesn't use the Row Headers option because that would also change the background of the Period field.

Period	Actual				QTD				YTD			
Region	Actual	Target	$VTT	YoY%	Actual	Target	$VTT	YoY%	Actual	Target	$VTT	YoY%
CENTRAL	$176,989	$154,005	$22,984	43%	$376,494	$339,635	$36,859	47%	$928,941	$339,635	$47,083	46%
EAST	$621,381	$507,861	$113,520	24%	$1,338,124	$1,132,024	$206,100	30%	$3,168,786	$1,132,024	$337,650	23%
NORTH	$437,552	$391,541	$46,011	400%	$792,711	$726,567	$66,144	342%	$1,514,295	$726,567	$25,077	237%
SOUTH	$178,089	$136,230	$41,859	1107%	$256,821	$191,890	$64,931	756%	$374,218	$191,890	$89,044	398%
WEST	$426,653	$349,042	$77,611	-52%	$893,938	$776,118	$117,820	-51%	$2,784,567	$776,118	$192,890	-40%
Total	**$1,840,664**	**$1,538,679**	**$301,984**	**13%**	**$3,658,088**	**$3,166,234**	**$491,854**	**10%**	**$8,770,807**	**$3,166,234**	**$691,745**	**5%**

Figure 5.9: Styling the matrix further.

Jim is pretty happy with the visual now, but he notices one important thing: The slicer on FyYear doesn't work. He needs to be able to show information for each fiscal year. Now Jim realizes that he made a mistake. Because he selected the CurrentFyMonth column as a filter, selecting any other fiscal year will not work because CurrentFyMonth is bound to the current fiscal year rather than to each fiscal year. He needs to find a different way to set this filter on the visual, so he decides to add a new calculated column that selects the last month for each year.

Jim goes to the Calendar table and creates the following new measure to select the last date for each year:

```
[Last fiscal month of the year] =
    CALCULATE(
        LASTNONBLANK('Calendar'[Date]
                    ,[Sum of Revenue])
        ,ALLEXCEPT('Calendar'
                  , 'Calendar'[FyYear])
    )
```

> This expression gets the last value for the Date column in the Calendar table for each fiscal year for which that date has revenue. Instead of using the ALL function, which would get the last value for the entire table, this expression uses the ALLEXCEPT function. The ALLEXCEPT function removes all filters in the table except for the columns supplied in the arguments. In this case, it will always give Jim the last period for the entire year; it will override months, weeks, and days but not years.

To test the new measure, Jim puts it into a matrix under Values and FyYear under Rows. Jim knows that the measure works because he can see the last date for each year.

FyYear	Last fiscal month of the year
2015	6/1/2015 12:00:00 AM
2016	6/1/2016 12:00:00 AM
2017	6/1/2017 12:00:00 AM
2018	11/1/2017 12:00:00 AM
Total	**11/1/2017 12:00:00 AM**

Figure 5.10: Testing the measure.

Jim now creates the following calculated column in the Calendar table so he can filter on it in his visuals:

```
[LastFyMonthofYear] =
    IF(
        [Year]=YEAR([Last fiscal month of the year])
        &&
        [Month]=MONTH([Last fiscal month of the year])
        ,1
        ,0
    )
```

> This formula executes for each row in the table, comparing the year of the current row in the Calendar table with the result of the measure.

Jim wants to test his calculated column, so he updates his matrix and adds FyMonthLabel under FyYear on Rows and the new calculated column LastFyMonthofYear under Filters. When he filters by the calculated column, it works as expected.

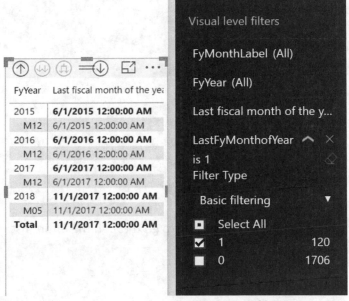

Figure 5.11: Testing the calculated column as a filter.

Jim decides he no longer needs the [Last Fiscal Month of the Year] measure for direct use in his visual, so he hides it in the Fields pane by right-clicking and selecting Hide.

Jim now updates the visual to replace the new CurrentFyMonth calculated column with the LastFyMonthofYear column as filter and tests whether the matrix now works when he changes the fiscal year with the slicer. He is happy to see that it does.

Now that the fiscal year slicer works, Jim wants to allow users to filter on other dimensions. He wants them to be able to see numbers by region and filter by device type, plan type, and product name. Jim plans to use slicers for this. Instead of using regular slicers, he wants to use dropdown slicers and add a search function. Jim starts by adding the ProductName field, which he changes to a slicer visual, and then he changes the slicer to a dropdown by selecting the small chevron symbol in the upper-right corner and selecting Dropdown.

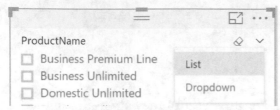

Figure 5.12: Selecting Dropdown.

Now he also wants to add a search function, so he clicks on the three dots in the upper-right corner and selects Search.

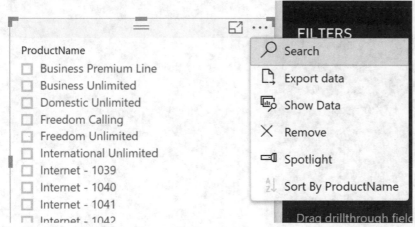

Figure 5.13: Enabling slicer search.

This means users can type a value they want to filter on instead of having to go through the entire list.

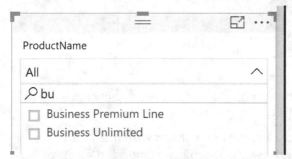

Figure 5.14: Searching the dropdown list.

Finally, Jim renames the field Product Name and turns off the Single Select option to make sure multiple items can be selected. Jim then repeats the process for the plan type and plan name. Jim moves them above the revenue matrix and uses the Format pane to make sure the three slicers are the same width. He then uses the Format pane to even out the placement of the slicers and align them to the top.

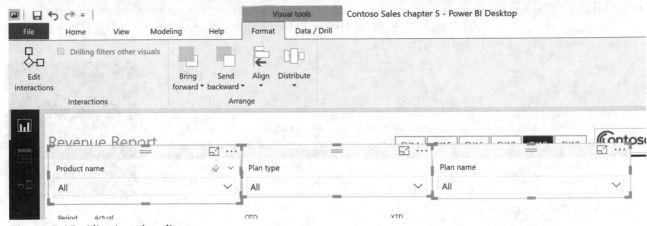

Figure 5.15: Aligning the slicers.

> You might notice that this report isn't designed the same way as the overview report. The idea is that a user can choose to go to a detailed report to see details and really dive into the subject area. The goal is not for the user to be in and out in a minute, as it is with the overview report. Still, some of the same rules apply to detail reports as to overview reports, such as making sure you don't put attention where it is not needed and ensuring that you align objects appropriately.

Now Jim tests whether the slicers work as expected—and they do.

Revenue Report

Data as of: 11/1/17   Reporting period: FY14 FY15 FY16 FY17 **FY18** FY19   **Contoso**

Product name	Plan type	Plan name
(Multiple Selections) ∨	Business VoIP ∨	VoIP ∨

Period	Actual				QTD				YTD			
Region	Actual	Target	$VTT	YoY%	Actual	Target	$VTT	YoY%	Actual	Target	$VTT	YoY%
CENTRAL	$893	$852	$41	21%	$1,946	$1,835	$111	24%	$4,994	$1,835	($131)	19%
EAST	$4,210	$3,849	$361	8%	$8,700	$8,027	$673	8%	$20,503	$8,027	$596	3%
NORTH	$1,205	$1,200	$5	315%	$2,325	$2,328	($2)	249%	$4,905	$2,328	($354)	143%
SOUTH	$485	$458	$27	362%	$697	$668	$29	255%	$1,087	$668	$40	118%
WEST	$2,646	$2,495	$151	-54%	$5,213	$4,996	$216	-56%	$15,494	$4,996	($130)	-49%
Total	**$9,439**	**$8,854**	**$584**	**-13%**	**$18,880**	**$17,853**	**$1,026**	**-16%**	**$46,984**	**$17,853**	**$20**	**-18%**

Figure 5.16: Testing the slicers.

To make sure the interesting numbers pop, Jim adds some conditional formatting to the report: Under the Conditional Formatting option, he turns on Data Bars for the Actual and YoY% columns.

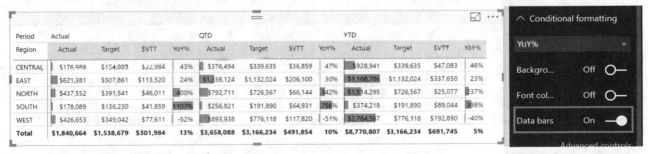

Figure 5.17: Adding data bars to the matrix.

In addition to showing the region, Jim wants to enable his business to drill down to more details and see each state. He therefore drags StateName under Region in Rows and clicks the downward-pointing arrow in the corner of the visual to turn on Drilldown.

| Period | Actual | | | | QTD | | | | YTD | | | |
Region	Actual	Target	$VTT	YoY%	Actual	Target	$VTT	YoY%	Actual	Target	$VTT	YoY%
CENTRAL	$176,989	$154,005	$22,984	43%	$376,494	$339,635	$36,859	47%	$928,941	$339,635	$47,083	46%
EAST	$621,381	$507,861	$113,520	24%	$1,338,124	$1,132,024	$206,100	30%	$3,168,786	$1,132,024	$337,650	23%
NORTH	$437,552	$391,541	$46,011	400%	$792,711	$726,567	$66,144	342%	$1,514,295	$726,567	$25,077	237%
SOUTH	$178,089	$136,230	$41,859	1107%	$256,821	$191,890	$64,931	756%	$374,218	$191,890	$89,044	398%
WEST	$426,653	$349,042	$77,611	-52%	$893,938	$776,118	$117,820	-51%	$2,784,567	$776,118	$192,890	-40%
Total	$1,840,664	$1,538,679	$301,984	13%	$3,658,088	$3,166,234	$491,854	10%	$8,770,807	$3,166,234	$691,745	5%

Rows
Region
StateName
Columns
Period

Figure 5.18: Turning on Drilldown.

Now a business can click on a region to see all the details for each state under that region. Jim notices that the region values don't fit in the column, so he makes the column wider.

| Period | Actual | | | | QTD | | | | YTD | | | |
Region	Actual	Target	$VTT	YoY%	Actual	Target	$VTT	YoY%	Actual	Target	$VTT	YoY%
EAST	$621,381	$507,861	$113,520	24%	$1,338,124	$1,132,024	$206,100	30%	$3,168,786	$1,132,024	$337,650	23%
ALABAMA	$37,419	$28,975	$8,444	-77%	$113,229	$101,466	$11,762	-66%	$477,784	$101,466	$25,081	-42%
ARKANSAS	$22,934	$17,925	$5,009	-74%	$61,830	$51,095	$10,734	-65%	$251,904	$51,095	$27,866	-44%
CONNECTICUT	$18,696	$14,241	$4,456	-46%	$56,103	$45,833	$10,270	-21%	$163,663	$45,833	$22,136	-8%
DELWARE	$2,985	$2,045	$940	-38%	$8,285	$6,830	$1,455	-18%	$24,033	$6,830	$2,124	-2%
Total	$621,381	$507,861	$113,520	24%	$1,338,124	$1,132,024	$206,100	30%	$3,168,786	$1,132,024	$337,650	23%

Figure 5.19: Drilling to a state.

The users can go back to see each region by clicking the downward-pointing arrow again.

Jim wants his users to be able to see the revenue by plan name as well, so he simply copies the region visual and replaces By Region with By Plan Name. He then spends some time aligning the visual and its columns. Finally, he adds a title above each chart by creating a text box with 0% transparency that describes what the chart is about; he then places the text box over the chart title. The newly added text now replaces and hides the built-in title of the visual (which cannot be customized).

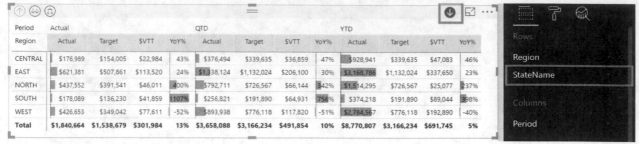

Revenue Report

Data as of: 11/1/17   Reporting period: FY14 FY15 FY16 FY17 **FY18** FY19   Contoso

Product name		Plan type		Plan name	
All		All		All	

By region

| Region | Actual | | | | QTD | | | | YTD | | | |
	Actual	Target	$VTT	YoY%	Actual	Target	$VTT	YoY%	Actual	Target	$VTT	YoY%
CENTRAL	$176,989	$154,005	$22,984	43%	$376,494	$339,635	$36,859	47%	$928,941	$339,635	$47,083	46%
EAST	$621,381	$507,861	$113,520	24%	$1,338,124	$1,132,024	$206,100	30%	$3,168,786	$1,132,024	$337,650	23%
NORTH	$437,552	$391,541	$46,011	400%	$792,711	$726,567	$66,144	342%	$1,514,295	$726,567	$25,077	237%
SOUTH	$178,089	$136,230	$41,859	1107%	$256,821	$191,890	$64,931	756%	$374,218	$191,890	$89,044	398%
WEST	$426,653	$349,042	$77,611	-52%	$893,938	$776,118	$117,820	-51%	$2,784,567	$776,118	$192,890	-40%
Total	$1,840,664	$1,538,679	$301,984	13%	$3,658,088	$3,166,234	$491,854	10%	$8,770,807	$3,166,234	$691,745	5%

By plan name

| PlanName | Actual | | | | QTD | | | | YTD | | | |
	Actual	Target	$VTT	YoY%	Actual	Target	$VTT	YoY%	Actual	Target	$VTT	YoY%
1 GB Plan	$24,206	$23,686	$521	2%	$47,814	$48,032	($218)	-1%	$117,668	$48,032	($4,087)	-5%
1 mbps Plan	$44,877	$43,066	$1,811	14%	$88,716	$87,806	$910	9%	$212,842	$87,806	($8,839)	4%
120 Minutes / Month	$24,845	$23,770	$1,075	6%	$49,281	$48,166	$1,115	3%	$121,142	$48,166	($1,944)	1%
128 kbps Plan	$39,763	$38,810	$952	4%	$79,692	$79,586	$106	1%	$194,303	$79,586	($5,965)	-1%
180 Minutes / Month	$25,288	$25,657	($369)	13%	$49,889	$51,924	($2,036)	8%	$121,220	$51,924	($8,298)	5%
2 mbps Plan	$18,885	$17,412	$1,473	11%	$37,135	$35,166	$1,970	8%	$88,748	$35,166	$375	7%
Total	$1,840,664	$1,538,679	$301,984	13%	$3,658,088	$3,166,234	$491,854	10%	$8,770,807	$3,166,234	$691,745	5%

Figure 5.20: Adding the visual by plan name with customized titles.

Jim wants the report to show another aspect of revenue: revenue over time. He decides to create a comparison chart that shows revenue for the current year, revenue one year ago, and revenue two years ago.

He inserts a line chart below the matrix and adds FyMonthLabel under Axis and Sum of Revenue under Values.

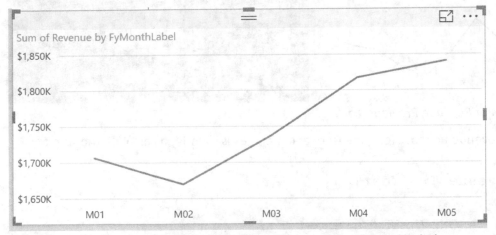

Figure 5.21: Inserting a line chart with Sum of Revenue by FyMonthLabel.

Jim wants to add sum of revenue for the previous year, but he is unable to find the measure for this. He then remembers that he hid this measure earlier, so he goes back to the Fields pane and selects View Hidden so he can see the hidden measures.

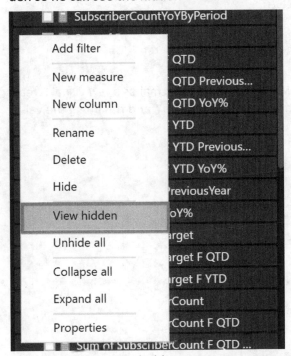

Figure 5.22: Showing hidden measures.

Now he can add the measure to the line chart.

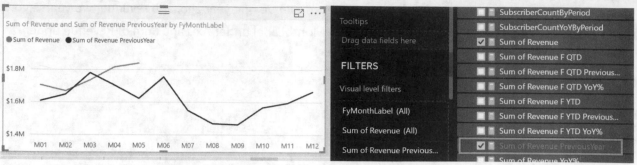

Figure 5.23: Adding [Sum of Revenue PreviousYear].

Jim copies the [Sum of Revenue PreviousYear] measure and modifies is slightly to calculate the sum of revenue two years ago:

```
[Sum of Revenue Two Year] =
    IF (
            HASONEVALUE(Calendar[FyYear])
                ,CALCULATE([Sum of Revenue]
                    ,DATEADD(Calendar[Date]
                        ,-2
                        ,YEAR
                        )
                    )
            )
```

Jim adds to the chart sum of revenue for last year and for two years ago. He also makes a few visual tweaks to the chart—moving the legend to the bottom, changing the title to Revenue YoY, and renaming the values.

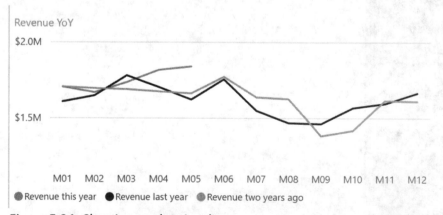

Figure 5.24: Cleaning up the visual.

Jim knows it's very important for the finance team to be able to project sales for the rest of the year. He wants to revise the chart to show a projection of revenue for the rest of the year, based on results in the past. He needs to use several complex DAX calculations to accomplish this.

> Don't be too overwhelmed by the DAX expressions in this chapter. These examples are meant to show you what the DAX language is capable of and to give you some ideas for your own DAX calculations.

Jim needs to determine the growth rate that he wants to use to project future sales. He decides he wants to use the average year-over-year growth rate for the past six months to project into the future. He uses the following DAX calculations to accomplish this:

```
[Avg GrowthRate last 6 months]=
  CALCULATE(
        AVERAGEX(
                ALL(Calendar[YearMonth])
                ,[Sum of Revenue YoY%])
                ,ALL('Calendar')
                ,DATESINPERIOD(Calendar[Date]
                        ,CALCULATE(
                            LASTNONBLANK(Calendar[Date]
                                    ,[Sum of Revenue])
                            ,ALL('Calendar'))
                        ,-6
                        ,MONTH)
        )
```

> This measure determines the average of [Sum of Revenue YoY%] for each 'Calendar'[Year-Month] for which the dates fall within the period up to six months before the last date in which there is [Sum of Revenue]. The AVERAGEX function ensures that the average is calculating the [Sum of Revenue YoY%] values for each 'Calendar'[YearMonth] value. The CALCULATE function allows the calculation to reach outside the current date context determined by the chart by using ALL('Calendar'). Then the DATESINPERIOD function adds a new context. This function returns all rows for the 'Calendar'[Date] column between the LASTNONBLANK 'Calendar'[Date] value where there is a [Sum of Revenue] and six months previous to that date, making sure to use the entire Calendar table by using CALCULATE and the ALL('Calendar') filter.

Next, Jim creates a measure that determines the number of months since the current month:

```
[MonthsSinceCurrentMonth] =
    (
        YEAR(STARTOFMONTH(Calendar[Date]))
        -
        YEAR([Absolute Last Invoice Date])
    ) * 12
    +
    MONTH(STARTOFMONTH(Calendar[Date]))
    -
    MONTH([Absolute Last Invoice Date])
```

> This function calculates the YEAR of the first day of the month, using STARTOFMONTH for the current 'Calendar'[Date] column and then subtracting the YEAR of the date returned by [Absolute Last Invoice Date]. The result is multiplied by 12 because each year has 12 months. The results are then added to the difference between the MONTH returned by the STARTOFMONTH function for the current 'Calendar'[Date] and the MONTH of the date returned by [Absolute Last Invoice Date]. This results in the difference in months between two dates. For more information on these types of expressions, see **http://ppivot.us/Zz1zb**.

Jim can now multiply the average growth rate by the months in the future. The more months in the future, the higher the number.

Jim wants to use the two previous calculations to determine the projected growth. He uses the POWER function to raise 1 plus the average growth rate by the number of months since the current month. This gives a nice trajectory for the revenue growth:

```
[ProjectedGrowthFactor] =
    POWER(1 + [Avg GrowthRate last 6 months]
        ,[MonthsSinceCurrentMonth])
```

> For a similar calculation, see this blog post on PowerPivotPro.com: **http://ppivot.us/CBiYi**.

Now all that needs to be done is to multiply the revenue from the last month by the projected growth factor. Jim determines the last revenue value for Contoso:

```
[Last Revenue] =
    CALCULATE([Sum of Revenue]
        ,Calendar[CurrentFyMonth]=1
        ,ALL('Calendar')
        )
```

> This measure uses the ALL function to determine [Sum of Revenue] where CurrentFyMonth is 1 for the entire Calendar table.

Finally, Jim can multiply [Last Revenue] by [ProjectedGrowthFactor], but only if [MonthsSinceCurrentMonth] returns a positive number, meaning a month is in the future:

```
[ProjectedRevenue] =
    IF([MonthsSinceCurrentMonth] >= 0
    ,[Last Revenue] * [ProjectedGrowthFactor])
```

He adds this measure to the chart and changes the projected line from a solid line to a dotted line by turning on Customize Series under Shapes for this measure on the Format pane.

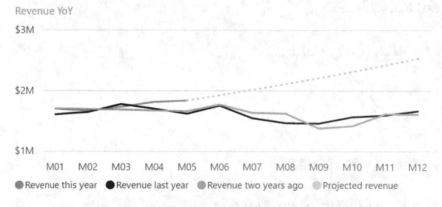

Figure 5.25: Adding projected revenue to the chart.

While testing this measure, Jim thinks it would be great if he could have the measure determine the average growth rate, based on a number of months that the user can select. Jim wants to add a slicer above the chart where the user can select the months to use in the forecast. He therefore adds one by using Create Table, with the values 3, 6, 9, 12, and 24.

Create Table

	TargetMonths	*
1	3	
2	6	
3	9	
4	12	
5	24	
*		

Name: varTargetMonths

Figure 5.26: Adding the new table to the model.

Jim uses this table in the model to add a slicer above the chart, and he also adds a title to the chart. He changes the format of the slicer to look like buttons again.

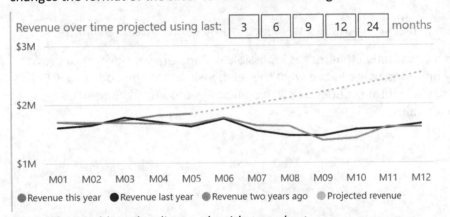

Figure 5.27: Adding the slicer and a title to a chart.

Jim creates the following measure to get the months selected by the user:

```
[getTargetMonths] =
    SELECTEDVALUE(varTargetMonths[TargetMonths]
              ,12)
```

This measure gets the value of `varTargetMonths[TargetMonths]` for the current slicer when there is only one value, determined by the `SELECTEDVALUE` function. If more than one or no values are selected, the measure returns 12.

Using this measure in the growth rate calculation is pretty straightforward. Instead of hardcoding −6 in the calculation, Jim uses [getTargetMonths] multiplied by −1:

```
[Avg GrowthRate last 6 months]=
CALCULATE(
        AVERAGEX(
                ALL('Calendar'[YearMonth])
                ,[Sum of Revenue YoY%])
                ,ALL('Calendar')
                ,DATESINPERIOD('Calendar'[Date]
                        ,CALCULATE(
                                LASTNONBLANK('Calendar'[Date]
                                        ,[Sum of Revenue])
                                ,ALL('Calendar'))
                        ,[getTargetMonths] * -1
                        ,MONTH)
        )
```

> This calculation allows users to play with the slicer to show the projected growth per month.

The last chart Jim wants to add is a visualization that makes it possible to compare year-over-year growth for the revenue to the number of units and usage to see what the relationships are. Jim adds a new line chart to the report and then adds FyMonthLabel under Axis and Sum of Revenue YoY%, Sum of Usage YoY%, and Sum of Units YoY% under Values.

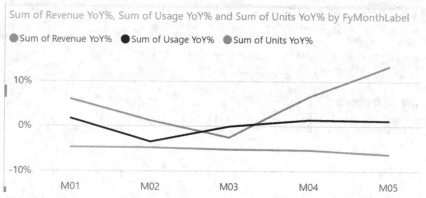

Figure 5.28: Comparing growth rates for several years in one chart.

Next, Jim moves the legend down to the bottom, adds a proper title by using a text box, and sets value names. To emphasize negative values, Jim uses the Analytics pane to add a constant line of a different color at 0.

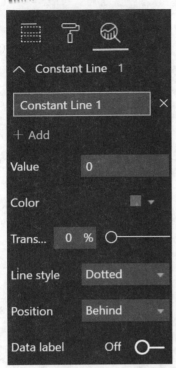

Figure 5.29: Adding a constant line.

The chart now clearly shows that percentage of units year over year is not doing well.

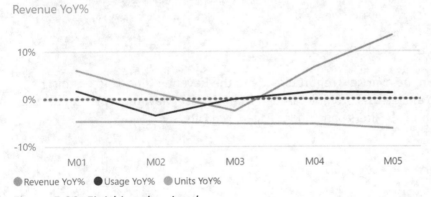

Figure 5.30: Finishing the visual.

The final report now allows users to dive into revenue from several angles.

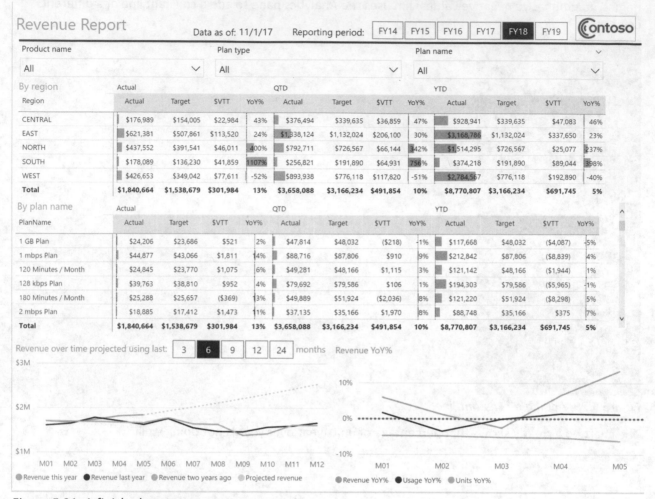

Figure 5.31: A finished revenue report.

Jim wants users to be able to go from the overview report directly to the Revenue report. To do this, he uses Power BI drillthrough filters. To enable users to drill through from the overview report to the Revenue report, Jim adds Region to the Drillthrough Filters pane under Page Level Filters.

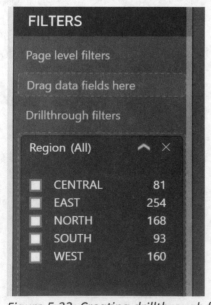

Figure 5.32: Creating drillthrough filters.

Now business users can drill into the Revenue report directly from the overview report.

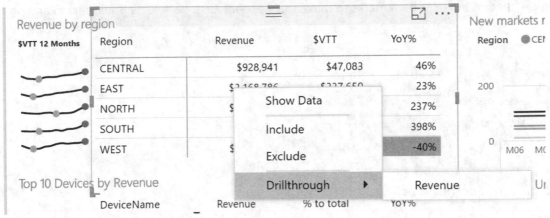

Figure 5.33: Using drillthrough filters.

Power BI Desktop Tip: Drillthrough Filters

Often business users want to be able to see as much detail as possible, but making this possible can be challenging, given the limited space of a report and the need to show the most essential information first. Luckily, business intelligence tools have had a solution for this since the early days: They have long allowed business users to drill through from a visual to a different report based on the selection on the report. Let's say there is a chart that shows sales by region for the current year, and the sales numbers are off target. This may prompt a business user to be curious about what is going on. A well-defined report allows the user to drill through to a report that shows the details for this number, automatically filtered for the particular region.

Power BI Desktop includes the Drillthrough Filters feature, which allows report authors to config-ure visuals to drill through to a different page that provides more details. For more information, see **http://ppivot.us/hfd4dfd**.

When a business user selects Drillthrough and then Revenue, the Revenue report automatically filters using the selected region.

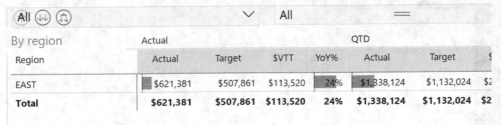

Figure 5.34: The filtered report.

Power BI Desktop automatically added a back button (a leftward-pointing arrow) to the detailed report, so a user can navigate back to the main report. Jim moves the filters to make space for the back button.

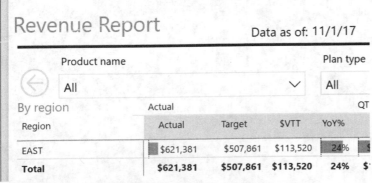

Figure 5.35: Making room for the back button.

Finally, Jim wants to allow business users to be able to navigate to the Revenue page by just clicking the Revenue by Region header. Jim uses bookmarks to make this happen. First, he selects Bookmarks Pane on the View tab.

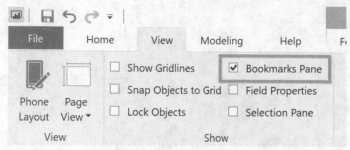

Figure 5.36: Opening the Bookmarks pane.

Power BI Desktop Tip: Bookmarks

Bookmarks allow you to capture and link to the state of a report, including filtering, or the state of a visual at a particular moment. You can later revisit that state from your report by selecting those bookmarks on the report page. Selecting a bookmark instantaneously sets the report to the previously captured state. This feature is great if you want to tell your users a guided story from within your reports (often called "storytelling"). It can also be used for simple navigation between pages, as described in this chapter.

More details on bookmarks are available at **http://ppivot.us/jgd3s2sh**.

Next, Jim selects the Revenue report and clicks Add on the Bookmarks pane. In doing this, he adds a new bookmark for this page called Bookmark, but he renames the bookmark Revenue Page. Finally, he deselects the Data and Display options because they are not needed for simple navigation bookmarks.

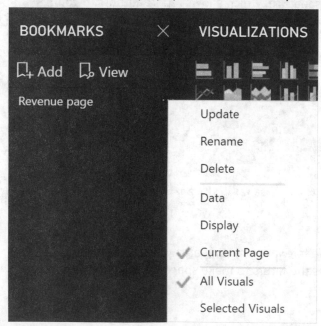

Figure 5.37: Bookmark options.

Now it is time to add the link for the bookmark, so Jim goes back to the overview report. Here he changes the format of the Revenue by Region header to Underline to make it clear that the user can click this header. Text boxes are not clickable by default, so to make the text clickable, Jim needs to use a trick: He adds a rectangle shape over the label with Fill turned off and Transparency set to 100%. This shape is clickable, and Jim can now set Bookmark to Revenue Page to select the link for the bookmark.

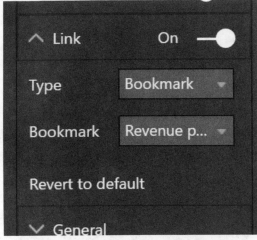

Figure 5.38: Selecting the bookmark.

Now business users can click on the label or click Drillthrough for the visual to gain access to a wide variety of interactivity.

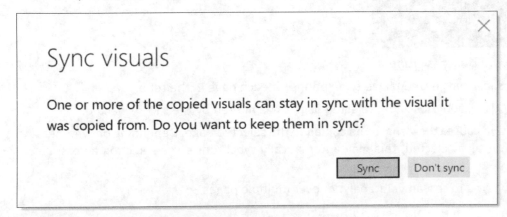

Revenue by region

$VTT 12 Months	Region	Revenue	$VTT	YoY%
	CENTRAL	$928,941	$47,083	46%
	EAST	$3,168,786	$337,650	23%
	NORTH	$1,514,295	$25,077	237%
	SOUTH	$374,218	$89,044	398%
	WEST	$2,784,567	$192,890	-40%

Figure 5.39: Enabling a user to find more information by drilling through or clicking a bookmark.

One of the great benefits of using Power BI is its amazing variety of visuals, one of the most powerful of which is the map visual. Jim decides to use the map visual to visualize regional sales.

Jim adds to the report a new page called Revenue by Region. He adds to this page the same header as on the previous pages by copying the header from the Revenue page. After he copies in the header, Power BI Desktop indicates that it has detected a visual that can be kept in sync with the visual it was copied from. Jim clicks Sync to ensure that whatever slicer value was selected will be synchronized between the pages.

Sync visuals

One or more of the copied visuals can stay in sync with the visual it was copied from. Do you want to keep them in sync?

[Sync]   [Don't sync]

Figure 5.40: Enabling slicers to sync.

Power BI Desktop Tip: Enabling Sync Slicers

Enabling slicers to sync means that report authors can sync report slicers across multiple pages. You can control this behavior by selecting the Sync Slicers option in the View tab.

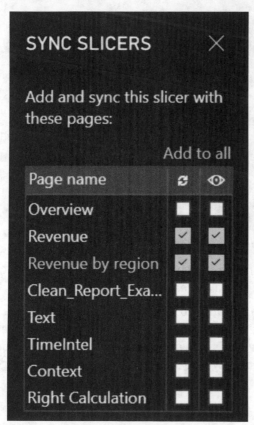

Figure 5.41: Enabling the Sync Slicers option.

With the Sync Slicers pane enabled, when you select a slicer, you can configure how to sync the slicer.

Figure 5.42: Configuring slicer syncing.

When configuring slicer syncing, you have two options for each page in the report:

- **Sync:** Enabling this option causes the selected page to be filtered by the slicer selected.

- **Visible:** This option causes the visual to be copied to the selected page. Depending on whether the Sync option is also selected, this may automatically synchronize the selection across all selected pages.

Slicer syncing allows you to spread your analytics over multiple pages.

Jim wants to show the year-to-date variance-to-target by region. He selects the Region field and adds the [Revenue to Target F YTD] measure, which automatically adds to the report a table containing these values.

Revenue by region   Data as of

Region	Revenue to target F YTD
CENTRAL	$47,083.2287
EAST	$337,649.929
NORTH	$25,077.2759
SOUTH	$89,044.3585
WEST	$192,890.109
Total	**$691,744.9011**

Figure 5.43: A table added to the report.

To visualize the variance-to-target by region, Jim decides to switch to a column bar chart. He moves the chart to the top-right corner and changes the default sort from region to variance-to-target by hovering over the chart and selecting Sort by Revenue to Target F YTD.

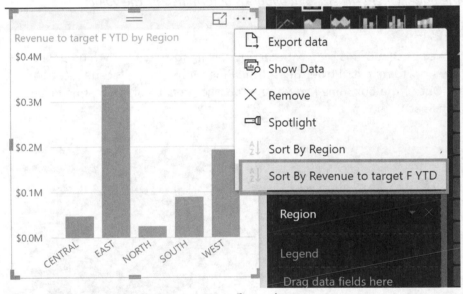

Figure 5.44: Changing the sort options for a chart.

Jim also wants to add his own text to the chart title, so he changes the title in the Format pane to Revenue to Target by Region and changes the font color to match the color of the header.

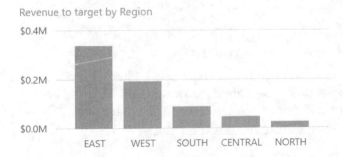

Figure 5.45: Cleaning up the chart.

Power BI offers a great visualization that Excel doesn't: a map chart. Jim decides to add a map chart to visualize the sales per region. He adds both StateShort and Sum of Revenue to the page and selects the map visualization. He then drags the visualization and places it next to the previous chart. Finally, he changes the title to Revenue by State and updates the font color.

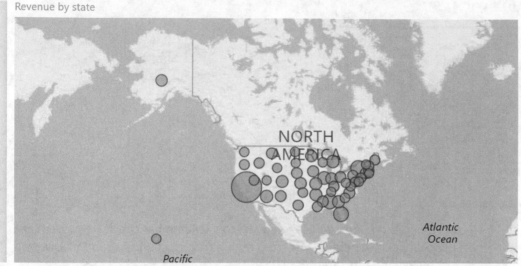

Figure 5.46: Adding a map to the page, where the size of a bubble is determined by the value.

Visualization Tip: Using Maps

It's pretty amazing, but Power BI shows this map without you having to specify anything about the data. How does it know how to map it? Power BI asks the Bing Maps engine for the location that you want to visualize. Out of the box, Bing knows how to visualize a lot of interesting locations, such as Safeco field in Seattle.

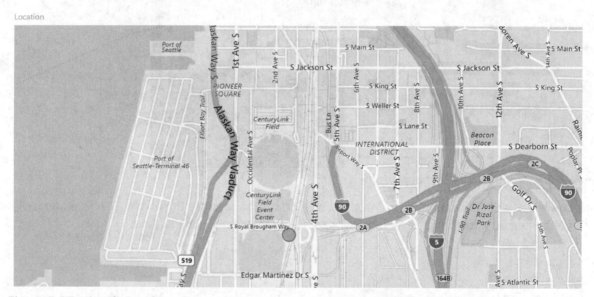

Figure 5.47: Visualizing data around the world—no latitude or longitude required.

Of course, there is one drawback to this approach: You need to have an active Internet connection in order to use Bing Maps. In addition, sometimes the data doesn't show up correctly because several cities or towns around the world might have the same name or other issues. This help document covers how to solve such problems: **http://ppivot.us/sfd6ma3**.

Besides the default map visual, Power BI also offers other types of maps, such as a filled map, support for custom shapes, ESRI maps, and even completely custom floor plans.

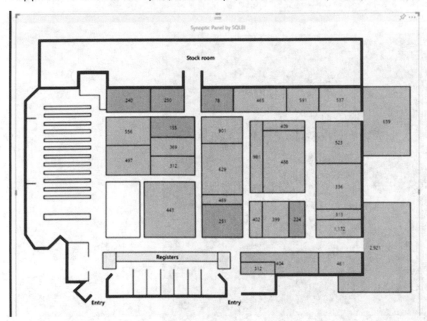

Figure 5.48: Custom floor plan visual.

The visual shown in Figure 5.48 uses the synoptic panel custom visual (see **http://ppivot.us/fdr3asd**).

Jim wants to highlight each region in the chart, so he decides to associate a different color with each dot on the chart, based on the group it belongs to. He wants to group the states by region, so he drags a region into the Legend area of the Fields pane; as a result, Power BI adds a legend to the visualization. However, Jim wants just the colors, not the legend itself, so he removes the legend by using the Format pane. He now has the chart he wants.

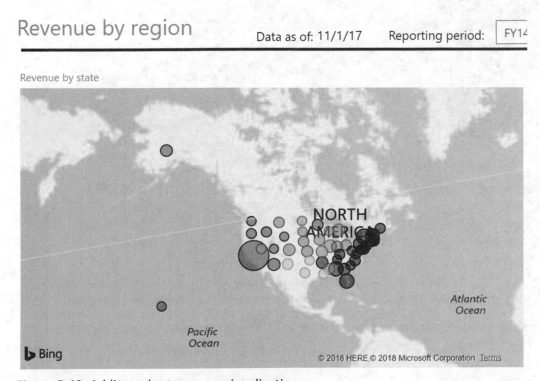

Figure 5.49: Adding color to a map visualization.

Jim wants this report to be as dynamic as possible, and he wants the user to be able to drill down to the city level. He therefore adds the City field under the StateShort field in the Location area of the Fields pane.

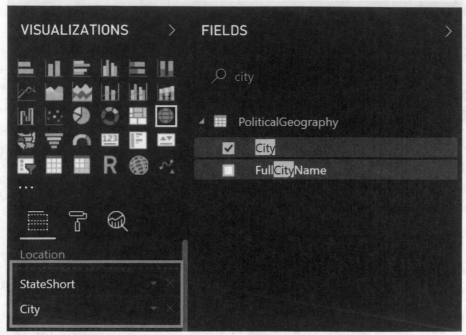

Figure 5.50: Multiple levels of location navigation.

Now when a user turns on Drilldown on the chart and clicks a region in the cart, Power BI automatically zooms in to show the cities that belong to that region.

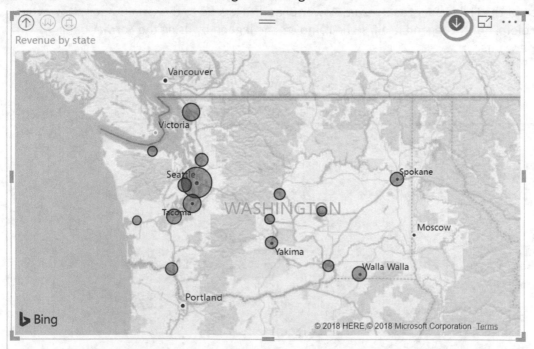

Figure 5.51: After zooming in to the Washington state region, the chart now shows each city that has revenue. The Drilldown button (the circled downward-pointing arrow at top right) enables this behavior.

At the top of the map, the upward-pointing arrow at the far left allows the user to navigate back to the region view.

Next, Jim wants to show the number of markets per month for the currently selected fiscal year. He verifies both the [Nr of Markets] measure and the FyMonthLabel column before changing the visualization to a line chart. He notices that the sorting is done based on the measure, and he decides to change it to sort by month, so he changes the title to Count of Markets and adds data labels by using the Format pane.

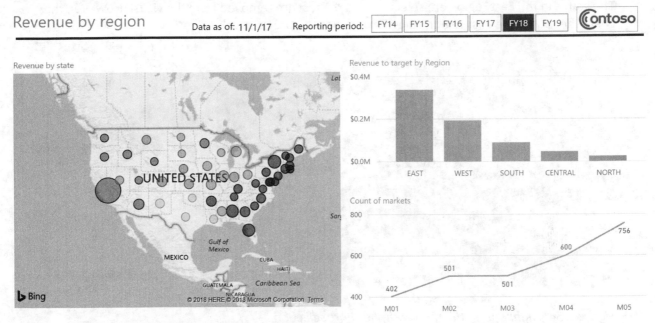

Figure 5.52: Adding more visualizations to the report.

Jim expects users to want to take advantage of the interactivity offered in the reports. It will allow them to filter the data by just selecting an item on the page. He therefore needs to show data in a different way than he would with a static presentation.

Power BI Tip: Cross-Filtering Data

Power BI allows users to easily bring data to life. They can cross-filter data by simply clicking a data point in a data visualization on the canvas, and Power BI automatically filters all other data visualizations on the same canvas. For example, if you click Minnesota on the map shown in Figure 5.53, Power BI automatically cross-filters the other two charts to show only the data for Minnesota.

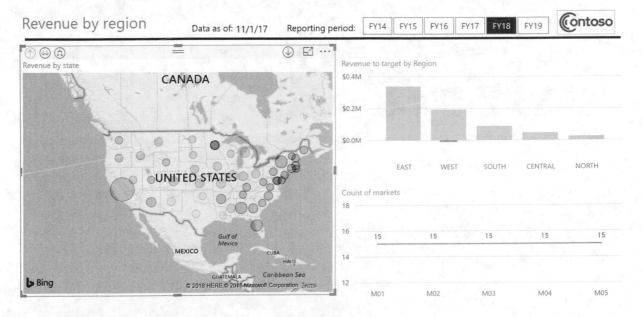

Figure 5.53: Cross-filtering the charts for a single region.

In the bar chart, you can immediately see how Minnesota is faring against other regions, which are dimmed but still visible.

Now if you click the East region in the bar chart, you see that other regions are dimmed but still visible, so you can still easily make comparisons. The same sort of thing happens with the map: The states in the East region are selected, and the rest are removed from the visual. However, the chart shows just the East region selection and not the previous values.

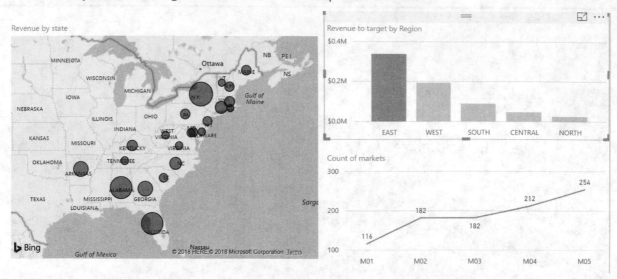

Figure 5.54: Highlighting the map with the chart selection.

Finally, you can combine the two features by pressing the Ctrl key while clicking on another item on the visual. Figure 5.55 shows the East region selected and New York selected while the Ctrl key was held down. Now you can see the count of markets visual filtered by both selections.

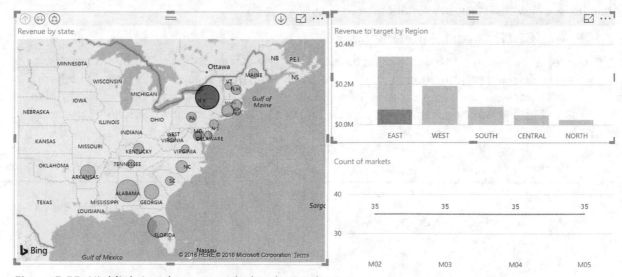

Figure 5.55: Highlighting the map with the chart selection.

This is great functionality, but sometimes a user wants to have more control and decide on his or her own which visual can be cross-filtered by another. Power BI allows this type of control over these features when you turn on Edit Interactions on a visual. With Edit Interactions selected, you can change which visuals get filtered through the selection of a value in the main visual.

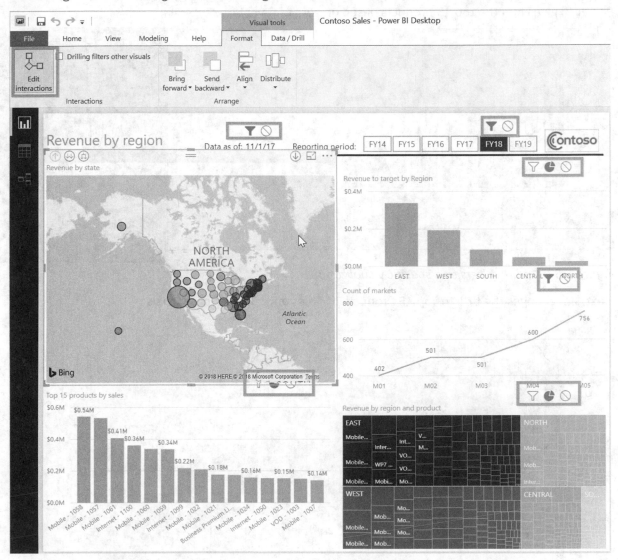

Figure 5.56: Changing the way visuals interact with other visuals.

Cross-filtering is an important feature that users love because it allows them to really play with the data. It is also a very popular feature for those using Power BI for presentations. A presenter can answer many questions on the spot by selecting values in a chart or adding filters to the Filters pane. Before Power BI, such information could be found only by going away to create another report and coming back later to show it to the appropriate parties.

Jim wants to be able to see the top products and the revenue for each, so he adds Sum of Revenue and ProductName to the page. Power BI automatically shows the best products first, sorting the visual by Sum of Revenue, in descending order.

Jim also wants to reduce the list of products to show only the products that contributed to the most sales—so listing the top 15 products would be great. He wants this filter to work for only this visualization, so he selects the Visual Level Filters area in the Fields pane. He then sets Filter Type to Top N, sets Show Items to 15, and sets By Value to Sum of Revenue (as the value to sort on). When he clicks Apply Filter, Power BI gives him the top 15 products based on sum of revenue.

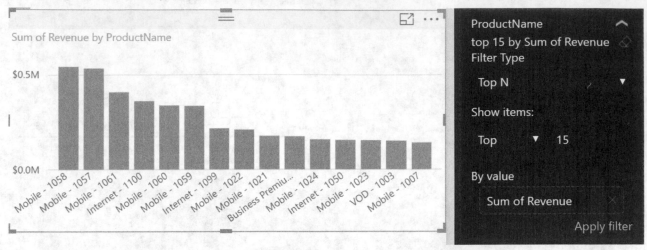

Figure 5.57: Adding filters to a specific visualization.

Next, Jim changes the title to Top 15 Products by Sales and turns on data labels.

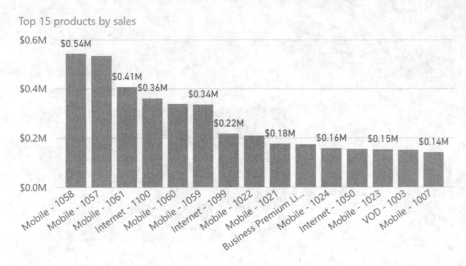

Figure 5.58: Visualizing the top-performing products.

Finally, Jim wants to give a visual overview of which product and which region sell best. A terrific way to visualize this type of information is by using a treemap visual. Jim adds a treemap visual to the report with Region as the group and ProductName as the detail, and he puts Sum of Revenue under Values. Then he changes the title of the treemap to Revenue by Region and Product.

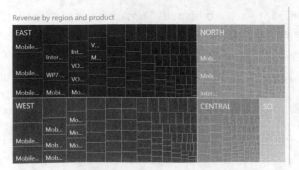

Figure 5.59: Using a treemap visual.

Together all these visuals offer great interactivity and instant insights. For example, when selecting a single product, a user can quickly see how well that product has sold in each region.

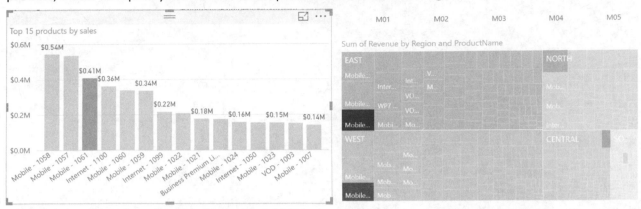

Figure 5.60: The power of Power BI interactivity.

Jim now has a dashboard with supporting reports that he is really happy with, especially for a first release.

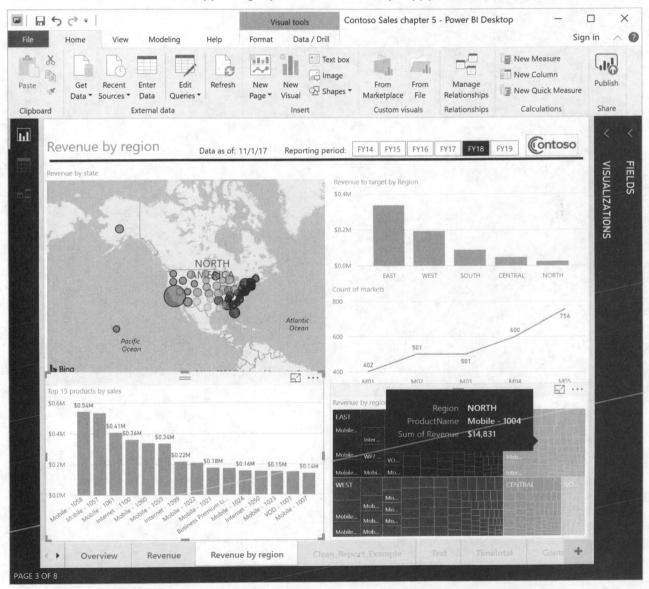

Figure 5.61: Jim's final report.

Jim now wants to share this dashboard with his coworkers and other stakeholders in the company. He will use the Power BI service to do this, as described in Chapter 6.

6 - Sharing Dashboards and Reports Within an Organization

Often the goal in creating a dashboard or a report is to share it with others and help them gain insights into the information shared. Microsoft gives you a few ways to do this:

- **Put it somewhere on the network or send it by email:** This is the traditional way of sharing data with others, but it has some flaws that are especially pronounced when using Power BI. Power BI can work with substantial amounts of data; it can create files that are quite large, and opening such a file over a network or emailing it can be difficult. Another downside is that not everyone is able to open a Power BI file because it requires access to Power BI Desktop on the local machine. When sharing reports and dashboards with business users, you should not expect them to have to install Power BI Desktop. Finally, the biggest drawback is that there is no real way of securing the data; you can secure a file, but you cannot use features like row-level security to tighten access to data. (For more on row-level security, see **http://ppivot.us/rlsfsd32**.)
- **Share it to Power BI:** Power BI (**http://www.powerbi.com**) offers a full analytical platform designed for analytics and collaboration without requiring the resources needed to install and maintain it on a local machine or network. Microsoft provides, manages, and maintains the Power BI service, which ensures that the functionality you need is up and running when you need it. Microsoft also continuously adds functionality to the service, without requiring the user to update software locally. We will look at using the Power BI service in detail in this chapter.
- **Share it to Power BI Report Server:** Power BI Report Server allows users to share Power BI Desktop files to an on-premises server. Power BI and Power BI Report Server both support Power BI Desktop files, but there are many differences. For example, Power BI Report Server doesn't support dashboards or apps, and whereas Report Server uses folders to store and secure files, Power BI uses workspaces. For more on Power BI Report Server, see **http://ppivot.us/pbirs2d2**.

Getting a Company Started with Power BI

Contoso Communications has decided to use PowerBI.com as its business intelligence platform because it will give the company access to the latest and greatest features. It will also save resources and money because Contoso won't have to maintain its own servers and do its own maintenance and patching.

Jim plans to use the report he created earlier as a pilot project for Contoso on PowerBI.com, so he signs up for a preview of the service at **http://www.powerbi.com**.

Figure 6.1: Signing up for Power BI.

After Jim signs up, he can log in to Power BI immediately, using his own username and password, because the organization already uses Office 365 for its email.

Power BI Tip: Integration with Other Products

Microsoft Power BI is natively integrated with many other Microsoft products behind the scenes. This means if your organization already uses products like Office 365, Dynamics, or Azure, it can leverage the setup done for those solutions in the areas of security and authentication. For example, it means the company's users can log in with the same usernames and passwords they use for their PCs.

If your company doesn't have Office 365 or any other integration, don't worry: You can just enter a password and get going! If your company later begins to use other Microsoft products, your IT administrator can then consolidate the usernames and passwords by doing an admin takeover, if needed (**http://ppivot.us/rlsfsd34**).

After logging in to Power BI, Jim is invited to add some data to it.

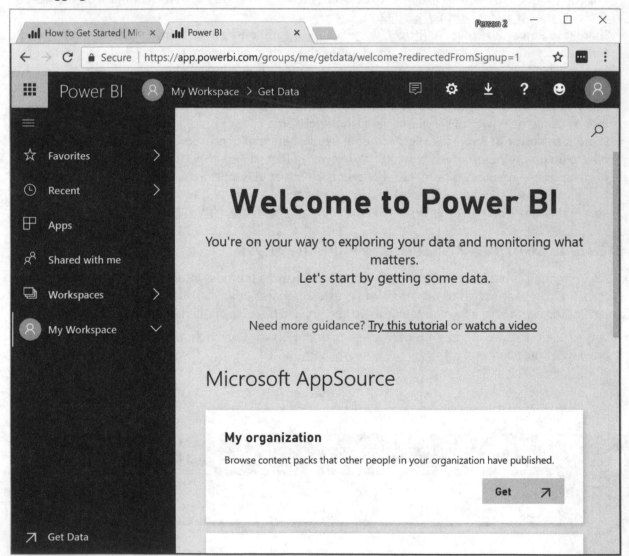

Figure 6.2: Power BI start screen.

Jim wants to share the report he created previously, so he uploads it to Power BI.

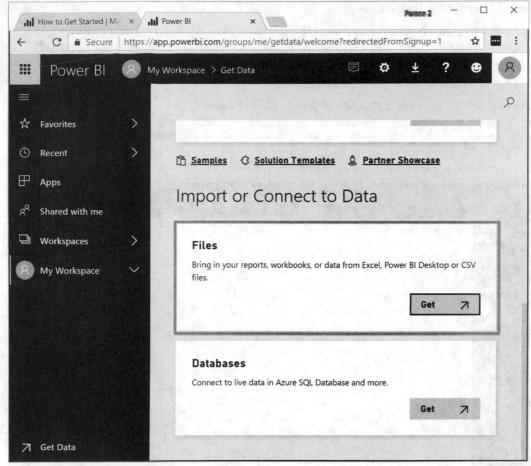

Figure 6.3: Uploading a file.

After clicking the Get button, Jim selects his **Contoso sales Power BI Desktop** file to upload.

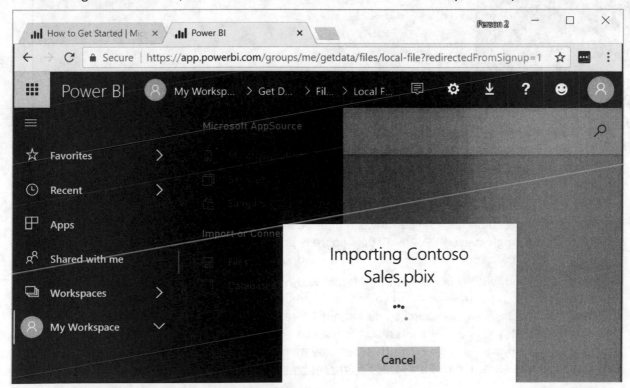

Figure 6.4: Uploading the Power BI Desktop file.

Power BI Tip: Publishing Reports

There are a few ways to publish reports to Power BI: You can either upload the files in Power BI directly, as shown here, or you can click the Publish button in Power BI Desktop. When you are signed in with your Power BI account in Power BI Desktop, clicking Publish is probably the easiest way to upload data to Power BI.

After the upload has succeeded, Jim sees a thumbnail for his file in Power BI.

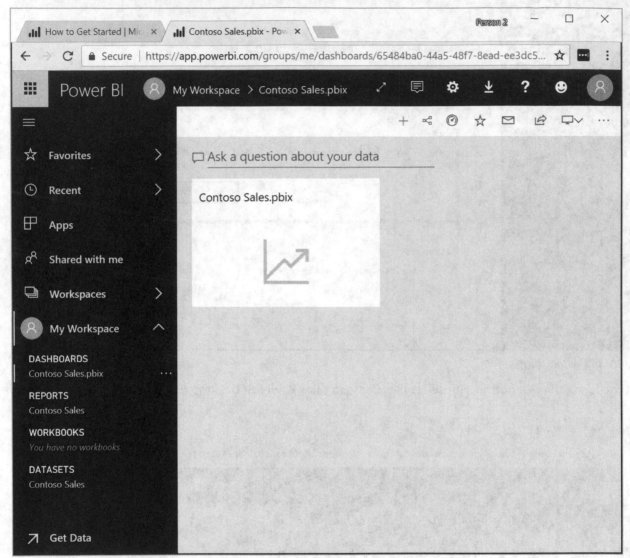

Figure 6.5: The file has been uploaded.

Power BI Tip: The Power BI Dashboard

In Power BI, a dashboard is a single canvas that allows data from different detailed reports to be presented in a single place. A Power BI dashboard is populated with "tiles," which are read-only snapshots of visualizations from any report in the workspace.

As you have seen, with reports you can interact with visuals to filter other visuals on the page. Dashboards are static, however, and you cannot interact with them because their data typically comes from disparate data sources and cannot be related in a meaningful way. If something in a dashboard triggers a user's interest, the user can click the appropriate tile to go to a more detailed report on the subject—and the user may be able to interact with the report. For more information on tiles and dashboards, see **http://ppivot.us/jsd5sf3s**.

After Jim uploads a new report, Power BI creates a new dashboard with a single tile. When Jim clicks on the tile, he sees his report, which is now hosted on the Power BI service.

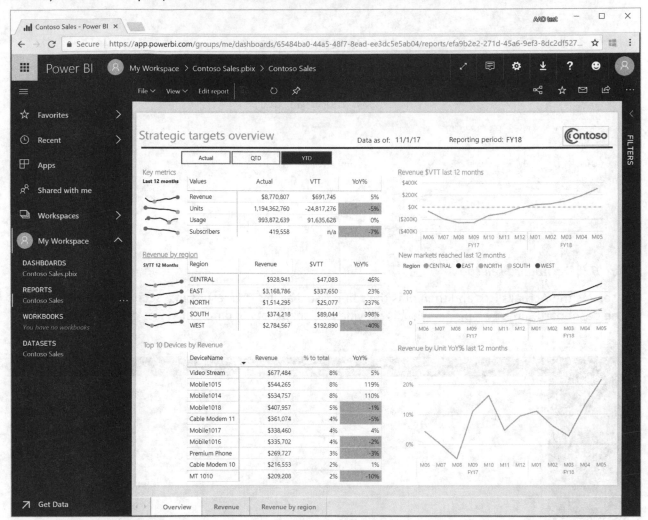

Figure 6.6: Jim's report is now hosted in the Power BI service.

The report looks and feels exactly the same as in Power BI Desktop, but it now appears in a browser window.

Now that Jim has browser access to his report, he starts designing the dashboard by pinning visualizations to it. Tiles will provide snapshots of the current selections. Jim wants to put the key year-to-date metrics as well as the current month metrics on the dashboard. He starts by selecting the YTD slicer and pinning it to the dashboard.

Strategic targets overview

Data as of:

Actual	QTD	YTD

Key metrics
Last 12 months

Values	Actual	VTT	YoY%
Revenue	$8,770,807	$691,745	5%
Units	1,194,362,760	-24,817,276	-5%
Usage	993,872,639	91,635,628	0%
Subscribers	419,558	n/a	-7%

Figure 6.7: Pinning the slicer visual to the dashboard.

Power BI asks him which dashboard to pin to, and Jim selects Existing Dashboard to pin to the current dashboard.

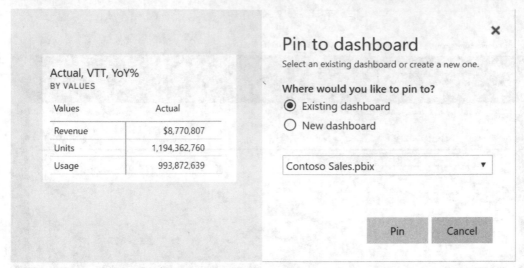

Figure 6.8: Dashboard selection.

Jim selects the Actual slicer and then pins the same visual again. This results in a second visual being added to the dashboard. Jim's two pinned visuals provide two snapshots of different states of the same visual.

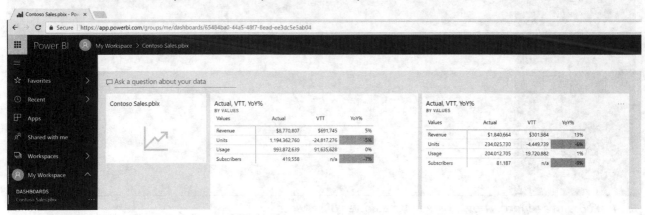

Figure 6.9: The first visuals on the dashboard.

> By pinning a tile, you save the current state of the visual to the dashboard. This gives you the opportunity to save any permutation you want. When the data gets updated, the visual will also receive the new data, as described later in this chapter.

Now that the first visuals are on the dashboard, Jim can delete the automatically created tile by clicking the three dots in the corner of the tile and selecting Delete Tile.

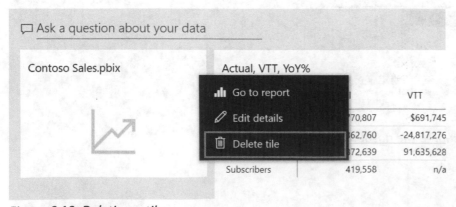

Figure 6.10: Deleting a tile.

Next, Jim wants to reduce the whitespace on the other tiles, but he soon figures out he can only resize the tiles to certain predetermined sizes. This means his tile cannot be resized much smaller than it currently is and retain its title.

Actual, VTT, YoY%
BY VALUES

Values	Actual	VTT	YoY%
Revenue	$8,770,807	$691,745	5%
Units	1,194,362,760	-24,817,276	-5%
Usage	993,872,639	91,635,628	0%

Figure 6.11: The information from the table does not all fit the tile.

Jim decides to add the title to the visual itself to save some space. He goes back to the report and clicks Edit Report. He then sees the whole report in the browser, where he can edit as he likes. In this case, he selects the metrics visual.

Figure 6.12: Editing the report in the browser.

Power BI Tip: Editing in the Browser

The Power BI service allows users to edit and create new reports in the browser the same way as in Power BI Desktop. Of course, the big benefit here is that users don't need to have Power BI Desktop installed on their machines. The Power BI service offers the same visuals and features for building the report, but there are some differences as well. The most important difference is that you cannot change the model in the browser, so you cannot add new measures or import new tables.

In general, I recommend not changing a report in the browser because from the moment you do, the Power BI Desktop file and PowerBI.com report will start to differ, which could lead to merging issues at a later stage. In this example, Jim is making some small changes that he is not saving, and this shouldn't be problematic. However, when creating new reports, you should start with a new report in the Power BI service (and leave the old reports untouched); this way, your reports never get overwritten. Finally, if you do make changes, there is always the option of downloading the PBIX file again; it will include any changes you made in the Power BI service. You can find this option under File, Download Report when editing a report.

In the editor that opens in the browser, Jim selects the measure on Rows and renames it Key Metrics Actual while selecting the Actual slicer. He then pins it to the dashboard. He does the same when selecting YTD, adding the second view over the same data. Back on the dashboard, he removes the old tiles. The new tiles almost fit, so Jim removes the display title and subtitle when editing the tile to make them fit.

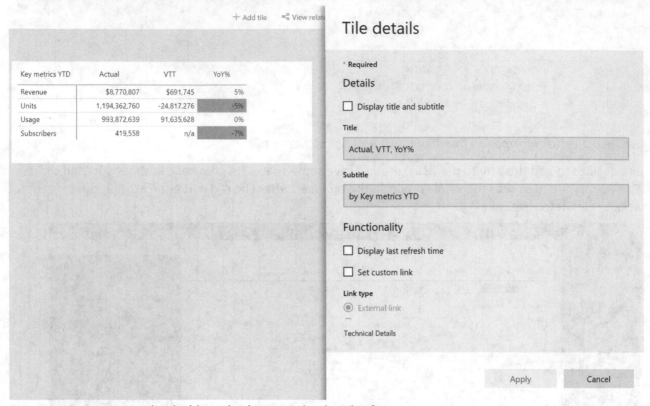

Figure 6.13: Removing the dashboard titles to make the tiles fit.

Now both tiles fit perfectly.

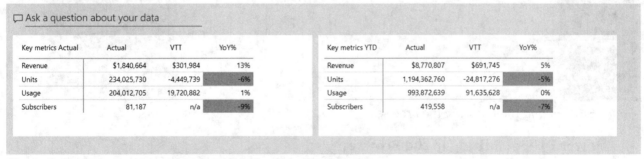

Figure 6.14: After the titles are removed, the tiles fit perfectly.

Jim adds to the dashboard several more visuals from the different report pages, making sure all the important topics are captured. He also ensures that all visuals look the same by aligning the titles.

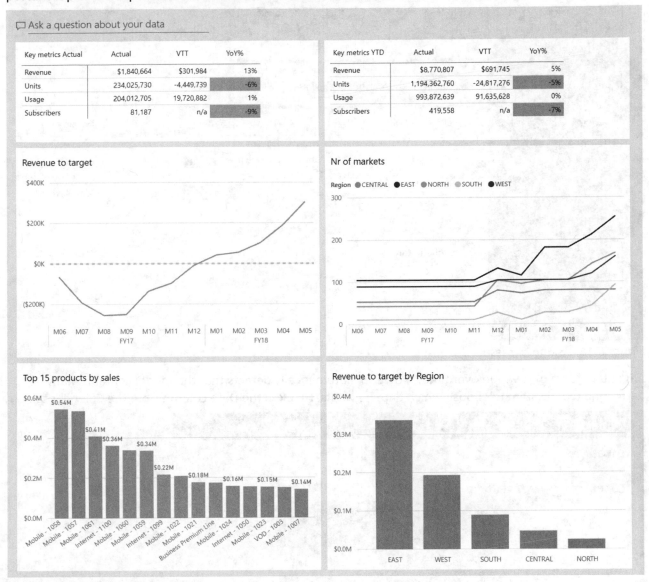

Figure 6.15: Adding all the visuals to the dashboard.

Finally, Jim wants to show a visual that displays the revenue over time. He doesn't have such a visual in the report, but he can ask Power BI a question about the data by typing text in the Q&A bar.

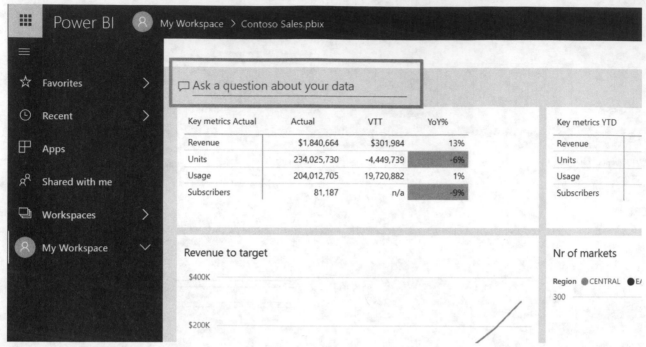

Figure 6.16: Asking a question.

Jim enters "sum of revenue over time." Power BI automatically detects that the model contains many dates, and it allows Jim to choose which date he wants. He picks the Date column from the Calendar table.

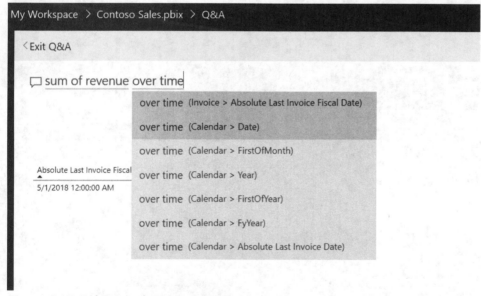

Figure 6.17: Selecting the appropriate column.

Power BI gives Jim a chart of the sum of revenue over all the time for which there is data available.

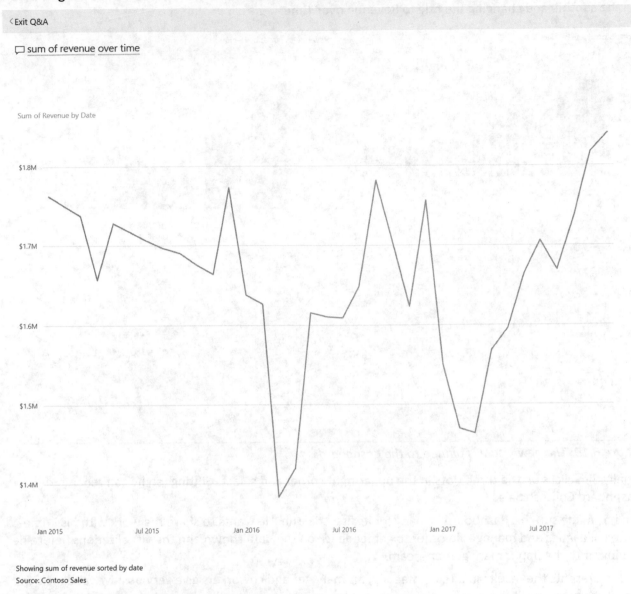

Figure 6.18: A visualization that answers Jim's query.

Power BI Tip: Power BI Q&A

With Power BI Q&A, you can simply ask questions (which don't actually need to be formulated as questions, as you can see in this example) about your data without having to drag and drop any data. The Q&A engine inside Power BI is able to understand your questions and apply them to the model you created. Depending on the results, it will decide which visual would provide the best format for presenting the information. You can use the Q&A engine in the browser or by double-clicking on the canvas in Power BI Desktop.

For more information, see this great help topic: **http://ppivot.us/hsaf3afs**.

Jim can now pin any visual in Power BI to his dashboard. He chooses one and cleans up the title by removing the subtitle and changing the title to Revenue over Time.

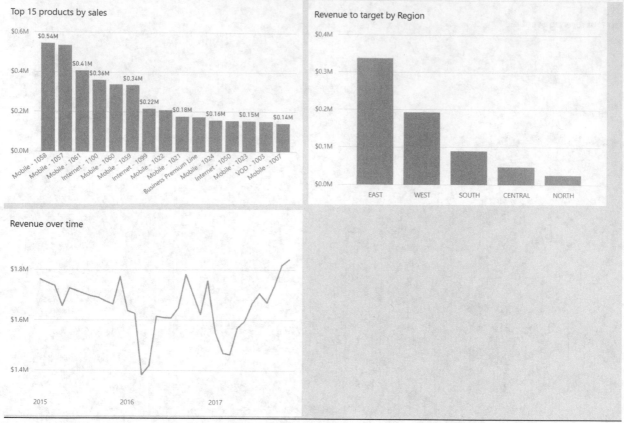

Figure 6.19: The new visual is pinned to the dashboard.

Finally, Jim clicks on the three dots in the upper-right corner and selects Settings so he can rename the dashboard Contoso Sales.

Jim has made sure his dashboard is ready for its first trial run. He wants to share the work with his immediate colleagues and manager in order to get feedback on the data shown and the visualizations before he deploys it to the upper management team.

As Jim presents the results in a team meeting, his manager and coworkers give very positive feedback. In fact, Jim's manager likes the results so much that he assigns Tracy, a colleague, to help Jim continue to deliver the dashboard and reports to the rest of the sales organization and management as soon as possible. What a big vote of confidence for Jim's work!

Now that Jim is no longer working on the dashboard alone, he needs a way to collaborate. He knows just how to do this: Power BI allows users to create workspaces that allow collaboration. Right now, the report and dashboard are hosted in Jim's My Workspace, where he can share the data with others but not collaborate. He needs to move it to a workspace where the team can work on the dashboards and reports in collaboration. To create a workspace, he selects Workspaces and clicks Create App Workspace.

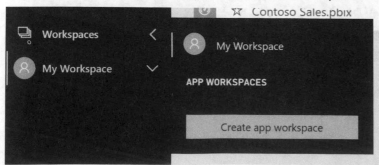

Figure 6.20: Creating a workspace.

In the box that appears, Jim enters details about the workspace the team will use.

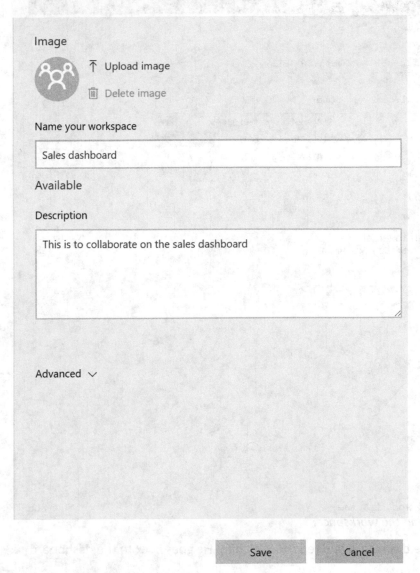

Figure 6.21: Entering workspace details.

Power BI Tip: Workspaces Preview

At the time of this writing, Power BI is changing how workspaces work. The current workspaces in Power BI are based on Office 365 groups, but this will soon change to remove the connection with Office 365. In this book I use the workspaces preview feature that is not connected to Office as that will be the new default going forward. Because it's a preview feature at this time, the layout and names that are used in this book might have changed by the time you read this. For more information, see **http://ppivot.us/wsv2pbi**.

Jim is again greeted by an empty workspace. He uploads the PBIX file again and populates the dashboard in the new workspace.

Figure 6.22: Re-creating the dashboard in the workspace.

Now Jim can invite Tracy to work on the dashboard and reports with him. He goes back to the dashboard and clicks Access in the bar at the top.

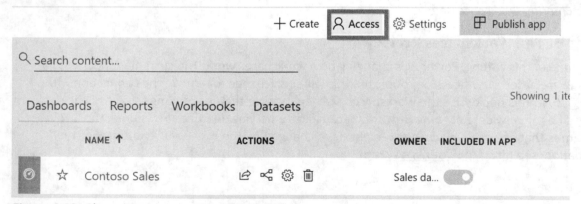

Figure 6.23: Changing access setting for the workspace.

Jim invites Tracy to the workspace by adding her to the workspace as a member.

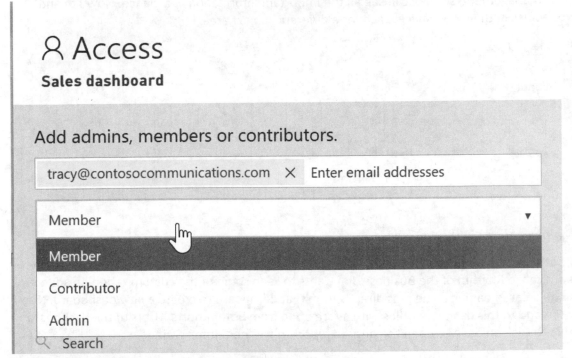

Figure 6.24: Adding Tracy to the workspace as a member.

Now that Jim has added Tracy to the workspace as a member, they can collaborate with each other on the dashboard and reports.

Power BI Tip: Workspace Access

There are a few things to know when giving users access to a workspace.

First, to be able to collaborate in Power BI, you need to have a Pro license, so as soon as Tracy gets the invitation, she will be prompted that she needs a Pro license to be able to work with Jim. Initially she can take advantage of a 60-day trial before committing to a full license. For more on Pro licenses, see **http://ppivot.us/prosd3s**.

Second, there are four different roles to choose from:

- **Admin:** Admins users have full access to the workspace and can even delete it or assign more admins.
- **Member:** Members are users who can update reports and dashboards, and they can share and publish apps, but they cannot make any changes to the workspace.
- **Contributor:** These users can only update the content in the workspace but cannot share or give access to others.
- **Viewer:** These users have read-only access to content in the workspace.

For more on workspace roles, see **http://ppivot.us/gd3eada**.

One of the first things Tracy does after being added to the workspace is to create a report on HR activities, which is another important area of investment for the company.

The HR data in this example comes from the HR sample provided with Power BI.

Tracy's goal is to create a new dashboard that combines data from both the HR and sales reports for the company's upper management, so they can see all the important information at a glance. Now Jim and Tracy have two reports in their workspace, each for a different subject area.

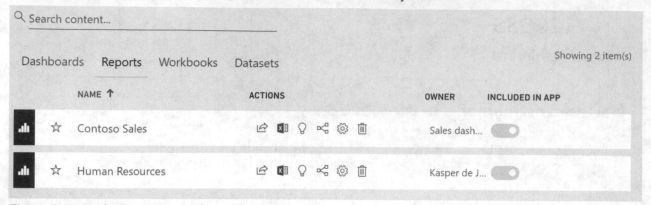

Figure 6.25: Multiple reports in the workspace.

Jim and Tracy both want to pick a few important metrics (visuals) from each of the reports and pin them to a new dashboard called Rhythm of the Business. Jim wants to keep some of the customization he added to the dashboard he created earlier, so he pins directly from that dashboard to create a new dashboard. Now Jim and Tracy can add to this dashboard tiles with information from both reports. Users of the dashboard will then be able to click on a tile to open the desired report to get more information.

Figure 6.26: A new dashboard with information from different reports.

Jim wants to make sure he keeps his dashboards and reports up-to-date. New data is added every day, and the data in the model needs to get updated. This doesn't happen automatically as the data is imported into the Power BI model, but to update the data, Jim can schedule a refresh to occur periodically.

Power BI Tip: How Does Data Refresh Work?

Power BI can connect to any data source that it has access to; it can be a data source that is connected to the Internet (a cloud data source) such as a SQL Azure database or Dynamics CRM, or it can be a data source that resides on the organization's network. This chapter shows how to connect to a data source that is directly connected to the Internet. (To see how to connect to a data source on a corporate network, see **http://ppivot.us/kd3as4s**.)

After Power BI is able to connect to a data source, you can configure the refresh schedule. At each of the scheduled times, Power BI will fetch from the data source the latest data and show it in the reports and dashboards. For more on data refresh, see **http://ppivot.us/vad4ed2**.

To configure this, Jim goes to the Datasets area of the workspace and selects Settings for Contoso Sales.

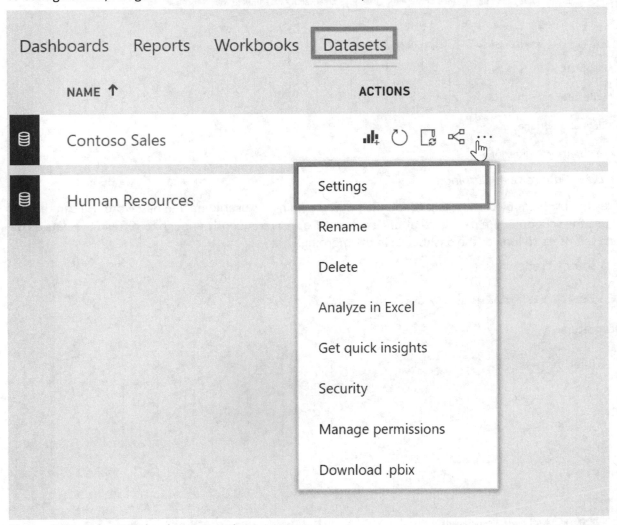

Figure 6.27: Selecting the dataset settings.

Power BI shows a warning that the dataset credentials are not set, and the data cannot be refreshed until this has been fixed.

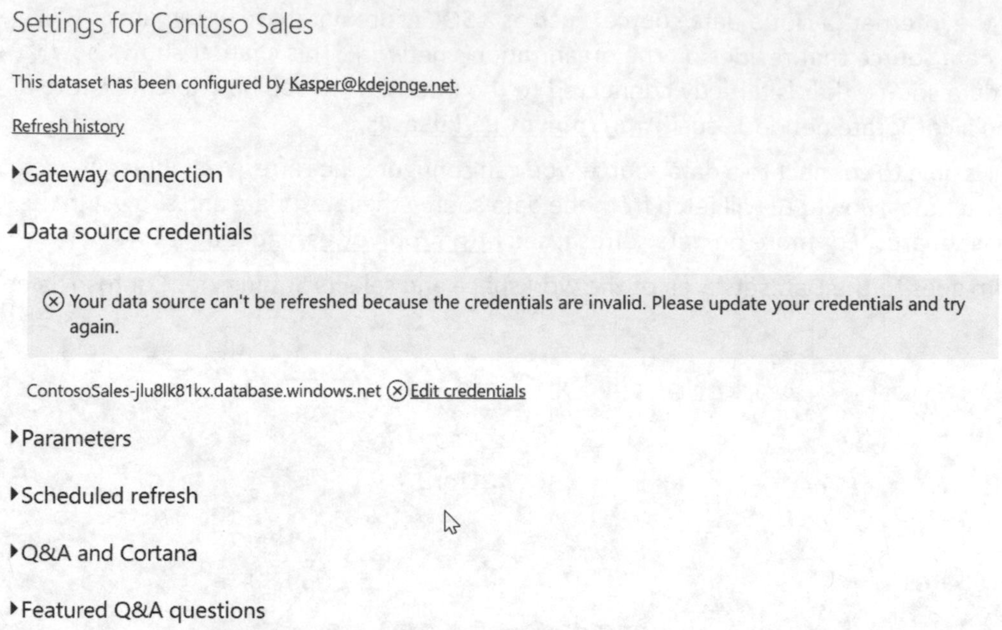

Settings for Contoso Sales

This dataset has been configured by Kasper@kdejonge.net.

Refresh history

▸Gateway connection

◢Data source credentials

⊗ Your data source can't be refreshed because the credentials are invalid. Please update your credentials and try again.

ContosoSales-jlu8lk81kx.database.windows.net ⊗Edit credentials

▸Parameters

▸Scheduled refresh

▸Q&A and Cortana

▸Featured Q&A questions

Figure 6.28: Data refresh warning.

Jim fixes the problem by clicking Edit Credentials and providing his username and password. He can then configure the schedule. Jim decides that once a day at 6 a.m. is frequently enough to refresh the data as he expects the users to look at the dashboard in the morning.

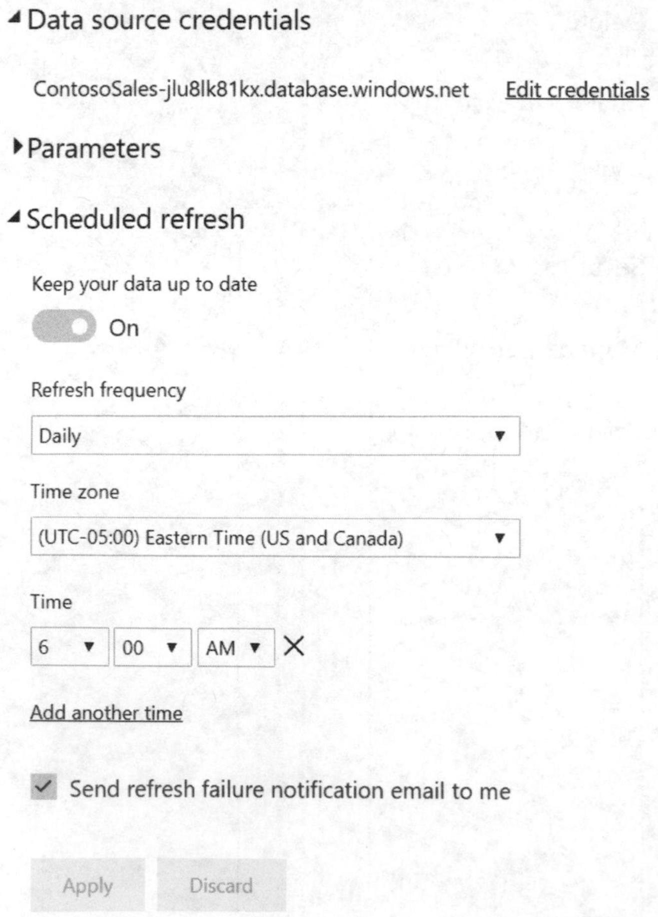

◢Data source credentials

ContosoSales-jlu8lk81kx.database.windows.net   Edit credentials

▸Parameters

◢Scheduled refresh

Keep your data up to date

⬤ On

Refresh frequency

Daily ▼

Time zone

(UTC-05:00) Eastern Time (US and Canada) ▼

Time

6 ▼	00 ▼	AM ▼	✕

Add another time

☑ Send refresh failure notification email to me

Apply   Discard

Figure 6.29: Configuring the refresh schedule.

He does the same for the HR system, and now his dashboards and reports will be updated every day at 6 a.m.

Now that Tracy and Jim have created the new dashboard, they present it to their team again and then make some minor changes based on the feedback. Now it is time to deploy the dashboard to some test users in their organization. They want to allow the users to view reports but don't want to collaborate with these users. To distribute these dashboards and reports to such users, Power BI provides apps.

Power BI Tip: Power BI Apps

Power BI apps allow a content creator to bundle related dashboards and reports together from a single workspace into a single app. The app can then be distributed to users in the organization in two ways:

- **Published to the app store:** An app can be published to the app store for everyone or for a set of users. A user who has access can select Get Data, find the app in the store, and make it available within Power BI.
- **Pushed directly to users:** An app can be pushed to the users directly, in which case they will be able to find it within Power BI immediately.

Remember that when you want to collaborate with other users of Power BI, they also need a Pro license. However, to be able to consume apps, there are two different options:

- **Power BI Pro license:** The user can have a Pro license. The organization might buy licenses for all consumers of the app. Often this happens when the company buys an Office 365 E5 package that also includes Power BI Pro licenses.
- **Power BI Premium:** A more common option is that a workspace can be hosted on a Premium version of Power BI. This means the organization pays for the capacity needed to run the reports and dashboards as opposed to purchasing individual licenses. This allows every user in the organization who has a free version of Power BI to consume the content. The drawback, of course, is that someone in the organization must manage the capacity. This option is most commonly used in scenarios where the users of the app look at the content only occasionally. For more on Power BI Premium, see **http://ppivot.us/pdghs3s**.

In some cases, you might want to share reports and apps with users who are not part of your organization. Power BI provides B2B (business-to-business) sharing to allow you to share an app with users outside your organization. This is great when you want to share information with partners or customers directly. Of course, it might also be dangerous if you have highly confidential information. Fortunately, the Power BI admin can determine who can use B2B sharing. For more information on B2B sharing, see **http://ppivot.us/xdfe4ss**.

For more on distributing and managing apps, see **http://ppivot.us/hsdf4sgf**.

Jim goes back to his workspace to create the app by clicking Publish App.

Figure 6.30: Publishing the app.

In the first box that appears, he can add a description to tell consumers of the app what it is about and who they can contact with any questions. Jim notices that the name of the app is the same as the name of the workspace, Sales Dashboard, even though it has grown to something more. He therefore cancels the app creation and goes back to rename the workspace Rhythm of the Business. Then he again clicks Publish App to create the app and enters the important details. Now the app has the correct name—the same name as the workspace.

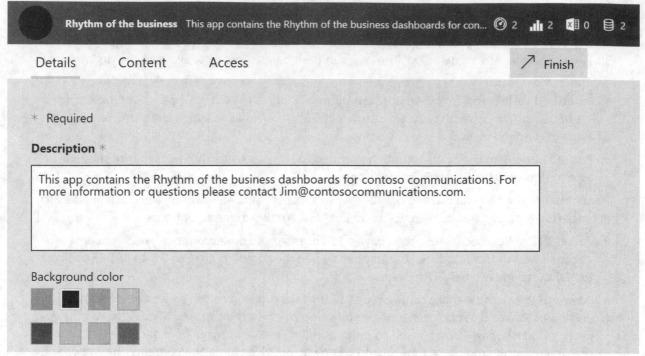

Figure 6.31: Setting the app details.

Next, in the Content area, Jim selects the app landing page. He wants to make sure consumers start with the Rhythm of the Business dashboard, so he selects it as the default.

| Rhythm of the business | This app contains the Rhythm of the business dashboards for contoso communic |

Details   Content   Access

App landing page ⓘ

● Specific content

○ None

| Rhythm of the business (dashboard) ▼ | * |

Content that will be published:

DASHBOARDS	REPORTS	DATASETS
Contoso Sales	Contoso Sales	Contoso Sales
Rhythm of the business	Human Resources	Human Resources

Figure 6.32: Selecting the landing page.

In the Access area, Jim sets the target audience for the app under Apply To. He wants the users to get the app installed automatically among their Power BI apps, so he selects Enabled.

Power BI Tip: The Power BI Admin Portal

By default, you cannot choose to install an app automatically because the Install App Automatically checkbox in the Access area is grayed out. Power BI has this feature turned off in the admin portal. You have to work with your Power BI admin to turn this on—either for the entire organization or for just a few content authors.

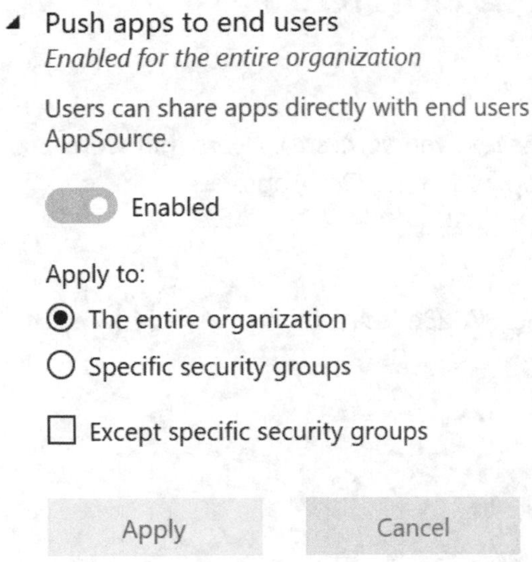

▲ Push apps to end users
Enabled for the entire organization

Users can share apps directly with end users without requiring installation from AppSource.

◉ Enabled

Apply to:

◉ The entire organization

◯ Specific security groups

☐ Except specific security groups

Apply   Cancel

Figure 6.33: Turning on the Install App Automatically feature by selecting Enabled under Push App to End Users in the admin portal.

For more details on the Power BI admin portal, see **http://ppivot.us/her3df3**.

It might be that your organization does not yet have a Power BI admin, and you or someone in your IT organization must tell Power BI who is the admin. This is called *admin takeover*, and it is described at **http://ppivot.us/4fsdad3**.

In this case, Jim is still testing the app, so he only selects Tracy and Ben from his team to get access to the app. He also has the app pushed directly to himself.

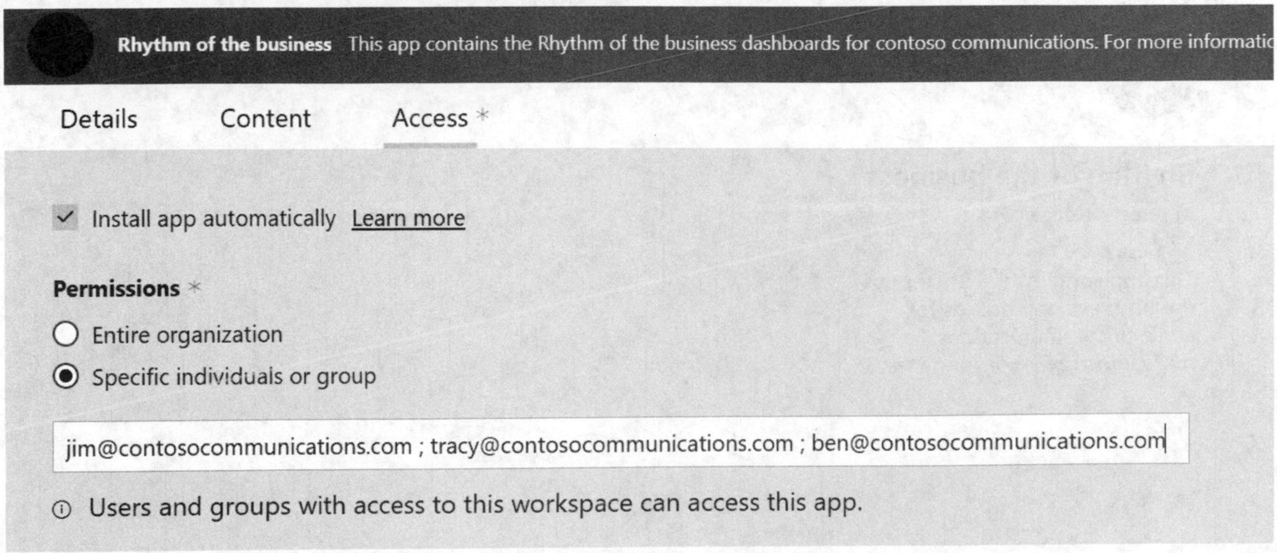

Rhythm of the business This app contains the Rhythm of the business dashboards for contoso communications. For more informatic

Details   Content   Access *

✔ Install app automatically   Learn more

Permissions *

◯ Entire organization

◉ Specific individuals or group

jim@contosocommunications.com ; tracy@contosocommunications.com ; ben@contosocommunications.com

ⓘ Users and groups with access to this workspace can access this app.

Figure 6.34: Adding users to the app.

When he is done making changes, Jim clicks Publish App again. Power BI tells Jim the app has been successfully published, and the users of the app can now find it in Power BI. The message also contains a link that Jim can include in an email for users to click on.

SUCCESSFULLY PUBLISHED

Rhythm of the business

You can now share this link with everyone you have given access to. Users that were given access can also install the app by visiting Get Apps.

-a9862db68c95&ctid=37ebcbf6-8053-4148-ab6e-67d28e7edc2b   Copy

Go to app

Figure 6.35: Successful app publication.

When a user who has access to the app clicks Get Data, he or she will be able to find the app under Apps for Power BI.

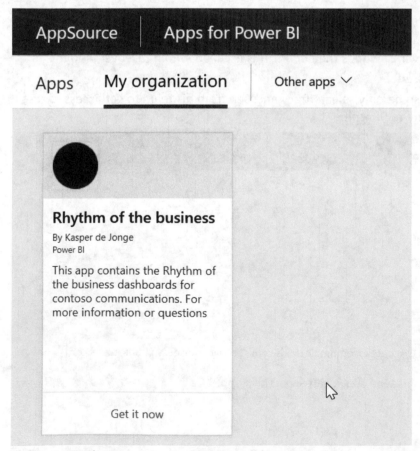

AppSource | Apps for Power BI

Apps   **My organization** | Other apps ∨

Rhythm of the business

By Kasper de Jonge
Power BI

This app contains the Rhythm of the business dashboards for contoso communications. For more information or questions

Get it now

Figure 6.36: The app as part of the Power BI apps.

Because the app was also pushed directly to Jim, he can now see it directly under his personal apps.

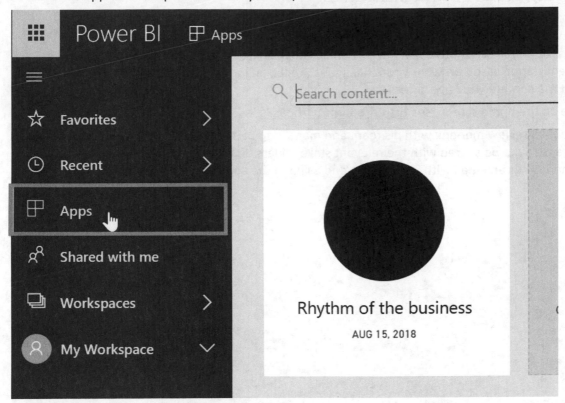

Figure 6.37: The app shows up in Jim's app list.

Jim can now click the app to open the Rhythm of the Business dashboard.

Power BI Tip: Updating Apps

When you use apps to deploy content to users in your organization, you are in control of when to update the content for those end users. After you make any changes to the dashboards or reports, you have to update the app manually. This ensures that you can send updates to your business users in a controlled manner and maybe bundle together a few changes on a certain day of the week. Remember that this data is being used to make executive decisions!

Finally, Jim returns to the Power BI home screen and notices that the app is shown there as well, so he knows his users will not have to look far to be able to see the app.

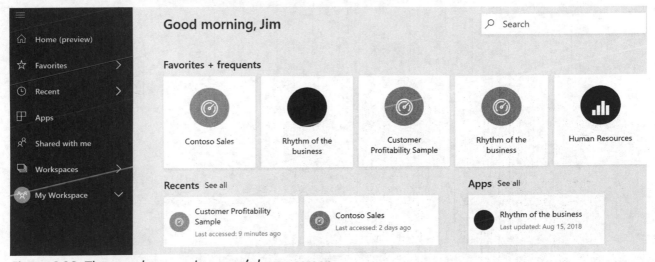

Figure 6.38: The app shows up in a user's home screen.

Power BI Tip: The Power BI Home Screen

The Power BI home screen is a central place in Power BI where you can find all the relevant content from recent and favorited dashboards, as well as available apps. You can pin multiple dashboards to the home screen to collect everything that is important to you. The home screen also recommends apps based on what your colleagues are looking at. Finally, it allows you to search across all the content you have access to.

For more on the home screen, see **http://ppivot.us/ho3s3s**.

After Jim has a final review meeting with his team and management, they declare that the reports and dashboards are ready to be shared with the relevant stakeholders. Jim shares the app with those stakeholders and then sends an email with instructions and a link to the app to help the recipients get started.

Index of Tips

Data Model Tip: Applied Steps and Script View 30

Data Model Tip: BLANK Values? 56

Data Model Tip: Comments 59

Data Model Tip: Creating and Managing Measures 54

Data Model Tip: Data Types 23

Data Model Tip: DAX Expressions 32

Data Model Tip: DAX vs. M 33

Data Model Tip: Editing a Query 21

Data Model Tip: Filter Context and CALCULATE 37

Data Model Tip: Formatting Measures 40

Data Model Tip: Import vs. DirectQuery 19

Data Model Tip: Making a Template of Your Measures 74

Data Model Tip: Query Editor Formulas 29

Data Model Tip: Remembering That Context Is Always Applied 65

Data Model Tip: Supported Data Sources 16

Data Model Tip: The Data Model 24

Data Model Tip: The DIVIDE Function 60

Data Model Tip: The Time Intelligence Functions 41

Data Model Tip: The VALUES Function 71

Data Model Tip: Understanding How Time Intelligence Functions Work 57

Data Model Tip: Variables 59

Power BI Desktop Tip: Bookmarks 106

Power BI Desktop Tip: Choosing a Version 13

Power BI Desktop Tip: Drillthrough Filters 105

Power BI Desktop Tip: Enabling Sync Slicers 108

Power BI Desktop Tip: Power BI Desktop vs. Excel 13

Power BI Desktop Tip: Preview Features 14

Power BI Tip: Cross-Filtering Data 113

Power BI Tip: Doing Short Iterations and Getting Feedback Often 48

Power BI Tip: Editing in the Browser 125

Power BI Tip: How Does Data Refresh Work? 135

Power BI Tip: Integration with Other Products 120

Power BI Tip: Power BI Apps 137

Power BI Tip: Power BI Q&A 129

Power BI Tip: Publishing Reports 122

Power BI Tip: Reports vs. Dashboards in Power BI 6

Power BI Tip: Slicers **25**

Power BI Tip: The Power BI Admin Portal **139**

Power BI Tip: The Power BI Dashboard **122**

Power BI Tip: The Power BI Home Screen **142**

Power BI Tip: Updating Apps **141**

Power BI Tip: Using Custom Visuals **62**

Power BI Tip: Workspace Access **133**

Power BI Tip: Workspaces Preview **131**

Visualization Tip: Bringing Attention Where Attention Is Warranted: KPIs **84**

Visualization Tip: Choosing the Right Calculation **78**

Visualization Tip: Choosing the Right Chart **64**

Visualization Tip: Choosing the Right Colors for a Dashboard **51**

Visualization Tip: Choosing the Right Precision **61**

Visualization Tip: Designing a Clean Report **48**

Visualization Tip: Keeping Space Around the Edges **53**

Visualization Tip: Labeling Appropriately **80**

Visualization Tip: Understanding Sparklines **63**

Visualization Tip: Using Fonts **51**

Visualization Tip: Using Maps **110**

Index

Symbols

4:3 vs. 16:9 52
// Comments 59
&& for AND 41
& operator 28
/ versus DIVIDE 60

A

Abela, Andrew 65
Add Column 28
Admin portal 139
Admin takeover 120, 139
Admin users 133
Advanced editor 30
Alice 7
Alignment 49, 75
ALLEXCEPT function 92
ALL function 39, 100
Allington, Matt 1
Applied Steps pane 30
Apply to Header 92
Apps 137
  Updating 141
Aspect ratio 13
Auto Date/Time 42
Automatic Calendar
  Turning off 41
Auto-size Column Width 62
AVERAGEX function 99
Axis display value 79
Azure integration 120

B

B2B sharing 137
Back button 105
Background color scales 85
Beautiful Evidence 63
Bing Maps 110
Bob 8
Bookmarks 106
Built-in date tables 42
Business intelligence
  Defined 1

C

Calculated columns 32
CALCULATE function 39
Calculation, changing 36
Car crashes 51
Card visual 73
Center align 61
Chart, right type of 64
Chart title 109

Clean report 48
Clickable shape 107
Close & Apply 31
Collaborate 130
Collecting data 11
Collie, Rob 1, 40
Color, custom 51
Colors 51
Column widths
  Prevent auto-size 62
Comments 59
Comparison charts 65
Composition charts 65
Compression 19
Concatenation with & 28
Conditional Formatting
  Data bars 95
Consolidate users 120
Constant line 80, 103
Contributor users 133
Core numbers 7
Create Table dialog 67
Creating a visual 23
Credentials 20, 136
Cross-filtering 113
Ctrl key 114
Current fiscal year 32
Custom column 46
Custom Column 28
Custom visuals 62

D

Dashboard
  Defined 5
  in PowerBI.com 122
  Questions to consider 6
Dashboards vs. reports 6
Data bars 95
Data Model 24
Data types 23
Data warehouse 1
DATESINPERIOD function 99
Date table 42
DAX
  Comments 59
  Variables 59
  verus M 33
DAX language 32
Decimal Places 61
Default summarization 36
Delete tile 124
Detailed reports 89
Dimension 24
Dimming columns 114
Direct Query
  versus Import 19
DISTINCTCOUNT function 65
Distribution charts 65

145

DIVIDE function 60
Don't Summarize 36
Drilldown by state 96
Drilling down 66
  Map chart 112
Drillthrough filter 104
Dynamics integration 120

E

E5 package 137
Editing a query 21
Editing in browser 125
Edit interactions 115
Else argument 56
Enter Data 67
EOMONTH function 44
Escobar, Miguel 21
Excel versus Power BI Desktop 13

F

Fact table 24
Feedback 48
Ferrari, Alberto 3, 40
Few, Stephen 50
Fields pane 22
Filter context 37
Filtering with slicers 25
Filter types 14
  Cross-Filtering 113
  Drillthrough 104
  Top N 116
Fiscal year 7
Floor plan 111
Font 51
Foreign key 24
FORMAT function 75
Formatting
  Alignment 61
  Chart x-axis 66
  Decimal places 61
  Headers 92
  Measures 40, 45
  Slicers 68
  Style property 56
  Underline 107
  Visuals 52
Formulas
  from multiple tables 34
  in Power Query 29
Freeform canvas 13

G

Gemini 2
Geocoding issues 110
Gestalt theory 48
Get Data dialog 16
Getting feedback 48

Goethe, Johann 48
Grand Total row 55
Granting access 132
Gridlines, hiding 87
Gridlines, show 48

H

HASONEVALUE function 69
  with Slicers 70
Headers, Renaming 60
Home screen 142
HR sample data 133
Hyperlink format 107

I

IF function 56
Import
  verus Direct Query 19
Importing data 16
Interactions, edit 115
Interactive reports 6
Interview 7

J

Jake 7
Jelen, Bill 1, 2
  Sparklines article 64
Jim 7

K

Kant, Immanuel 48
Keep related data close 49
Key metric 75
Key performance indicators 84
Keys
  foreign versus primary 24
Kimball, Ralph 24
KPI 84
  Defined 5

L

Last check 87
LASTDATE function 34
Last invoice date 33
Last month per year 92
LASTNONBLANK function 99
Legend location 98
Line, constant 80
Line, Separator 52

M

Map chart 110
Matrix visual 35
Measure
  Naming 54
Measures 32

Creating 53
Hiding 58
Managing 54
Number format 54
Reusing 54
View Hidden 97
Measures, Formatting 40
Member users 133
Memory limit 19
Metrics 8
Microsoft Store 13
MIT 51
M language 29
M lanuguage
 verus DAX 33
MOLAP 24
MONTH function 99
MrExcel 2

N

Navigation bookmark 106
Nudge 52
Number format 54
 with FORMAT 75
Number.ToText 28

O

Office 365
 E5 License 137
Office 365 integration 120
One-to-many 24
On-premises server 119

P

Pages
 Deleting 45
Page size 52
Paint roller 52
Past 12 months 43
Percent of total 82
Pin to dashboard 123
Power BI
 Release date 3
 Signing up 119
Power BI Apps 137
PowerBI.com 11
 vs. Desktop 3
Power BI Desktop
 Installing 11
 Versus Excel 13
Power BI Premium 3
Power BI service 119
POWER function 100
Power Query 21
 Custom column 46
Precision 61
Premium 137

Preview features 14
Previous Year 56
Primary key 24
Projected revenue 100
Project Gemini 2
Pro license 133
Proximity 49
Publish App 137
Publishing reports 122
Puls, Ken 21

Q

Q&&A bar 128
Q&&A in Desktop 129
QTD 67
Query Editor 27

R

Refreshing data 44
 from cloud 135
 Scheduled 136
RELATED function 33
Relationship charts 65
Relationships icon 25
Reporting services 6
Reports vs. dashboards 6
Revenue to target 78
Rhythm of the business 73, 134
RIGHT function in Excel 47
Row-level security 119
Running 12 months 44
Russo, Marco 3, 40

S

SAMEPERIODLASTYEAR function 83
Sample file 11
Scheduled refresh 136
Script view 30
Search function 94
Segoe UI 51
SELECTEDVALUE function 56, 75
Server name 20
Shape 52
Sharing dashboards 119
Sigma symbol 35
Slicer 25
 Appear as buttons 90
 as drop-down 94
 Single select 68
 Sync pages 107
Snap to Grid 48
Snowflake schema 24
Sort by column 74
Sorting charts 109
Space between 53
Sparkline 62
 within matrix 64

SSAS 2
SSAS multidimensional engine 24
Star schema 24
STARTOFMONTH function 99
Static report 6
Style property 56
Subtotals
   Hiding 91
SUM function 54
SWITCH function 70, 72
Sync slicers 107
Synoptic panel 111

T

Target months 100
Text box 50
Text.End Function 47
Text.PadStart function 47
Theme 51
Theresa 8
Thousands 79
Tiles 122
   Removing titles 126
   Sizing 125
Time Intelligence
   Golden rules 41
   How they work 57
Title from text box 50
Title of the visual 96
Top N filter 116
Top products 81
Tracy 130
Traffic light 84
Trailing 12 months 43
Transparent shape 107
Treemap visual 116
Tufte, Edward 63

U

Underline format 107
Updating apps 141

V

VALUES function 71
Variables 59
Variance-to-target 55
Versions of Power BI Desktop 13
VertiPaq engine 19
Viewer users 133
View Hidden 97
Visuals
   Creating 23
VLOOKUP 2
VLOOKUP versus Data Model 24
VTT 52

W

Webb, Chris 21
Whitespace 53
Win/loss sparkline 63
Workspace 122
   Access 132
   Creating 130

Y

YEAR function 99
Year-over-year 60
Year-over-year growth 69
YoY 52
YTD 67

Learn DAX in Power BI from Matt Allington

Supercharge Power BI
Power BI is Better When You Learn To Write DAX

Matt Allington

Learn Power Query in Power BI

MASTER YOUR DATA
WITH Excel and Power BI

Leveraging Power Query to Get & Transform your Task Flow

Formerly 'M is for Data Monkey'

2ND EDITION

by **Ken Puls and Miguel Escobar**